H. A. IRONSIDE
MEMORIAL LIBRARY

W9-BUZ-027

THE
SOCIAL AND POLITICAL
IDEAS OF SOME GREAT
MEDIÆVAL THINKERS

Works Edited by
F. J. C. HEARNSHAW, M.A., LL.D.
In Uniform Style and Binding

THE
SOCIAL AND POLITICAL IDEAS OF SOME GREAT MEDIÆVAL THINKERS

A SERIES OF LECTURES DELIVERED AT KING'S COLLEGE UNIVERSITY OF LONDON

EDITED BY

F. J. C. HEARNSHAW M.A. LL.D.

PROFESSOR OF MEDIÆVAL HISTORY IN THE
UNIVERSITY OF LONDON

NEW YORK

BARNES & NOBLE, INC.

First published 1928
Reprinted 1950 by special arrangement with
GEORGE G. HARRAP & CO., LTD.
39-41 Parker Street, Kingsway, London, W.C. 2

Printed in the United States of America

4278

PREFACE

THE course of lectures issued in this volume was delivered publicly in King's College, London, during the autumn of 1922. It proved to be an exceptionally attractive course, and those who planned it had the satisfaction of seeing the lecture-room filled to overflowing week by week. The regular attendance of the large audience, the evident interest with which all present followed the arguments of the speakers, and the warm appreciation manifested, all served to show that both the Middle Ages and Political Ideas are subjects concerning which a growing number of people are eager to be informed. It is hoped that in their present more permanent form the lectures will reach a far vaster audience than that which originally heard them delivered, and that on both sides of the Atlantic they may serve to introduce students to thinkers who have moulded the minds of the race, and to ideas that have been powerfully operative in history.

The lectures, with two exceptions, are printed substantially as they were first given. The two exceptions are those on St Augustine and Wycliffe. In the first case, the lecturer, Dr A. J. Carlyle, was unfortunately prevented at the last moment by illness from delivering his discourse. Hence, at very short notice, it fell to the lot of the editor of this volume to give a superficial survey of the circumstances which called forth *The City of God*, and the line of argument which the great Latin Father followed in his remarkable apologia. Dr Carlyle

5

was good enough, on his recovery, to dictate a summary of the address which he had intended to give, and that summary is included in this volume. As, however, it is brief, and as it covers entirely different ground from that which the editor traversed in his remarks, the latter has ventured to write down a *résumé* of what he said, and to include that as well. In the case of Wycliffe, the lecturer found himself so completely overwhelmed by the masses of his material that he was compelled, in mercy to his audience, to content himself in his lecture with a cursory sketch of the leading points, delivered from outline notes, postponing the more detailed treatment to the subsequent seclusion of his study and the leisure of the Christmas vacation.

For the guidance of those who wish to pursue further their study of mediæval ideas—and the main use of lectures such as these is to stimulate and to guide—the lecturers have provided brief bibliographies.

F. J. C. HEARNSHAW

King's College
University of London
January 1923

CONTENTS

7

THE SOCIAL AND POLITICAL IDEAS OF SOME GREAT MEDIÆVAL THINKERS

I

INTRODUCTORY

MEDIÆVAL POLITICAL THOUGHT

THE political theory of the Middle Ages may sometimes appear like a desert, often disturbed by the sandstorms raised by the conflicting genies of Papacy and Empire, and rarely relieved by a green oasis such as Dante's treatise *On Monarchy* or Marsilio's *Defender of the Peace*. There is, indeed, a vast expanse of arid writing ; and a certain unreality, as of a mirage, hangs over the expanse. The writers are untrained and unversed in politics : if they handle real issues, they have not lived in realities. They seem like students, writing essays on political theory from text-books ; and they are confused by the multiplicity and diversity of the three texts they use—the Bible, resting on Jewish theocracy ; Roman Law, issuing from imperial autocracy ; and the *Politics* of Aristotle, based on the oligarchies and democracies of the ancient Greek city-states. They do not realise the facts of the present, because they move in the theories of the past. In a Europe divided into many feudal states, they speak of a single undivided Empire : to a society revolutionised by the presence, and indeed the

9

dominance, of the Christian Church they apply the canons of an antique polity in which no Church existed and the State enfolded all life.

And yet we are looking to-day, and sometimes looking with longing eyes, to the theories and beliefs of the Middle Ages, as if they had secrets and suggestions for our modern life which must at all costs be recovered. Gierke, in a significant sentence, speaks of Leibniz as one " who in so many directions went deeper than his contemporaries, and who, perhaps for that reason, so often turned his eyes backward toward mediæval ways of thought." Whether or no the Guild Socialists go deeper than their contemporaries, they are like Leibniz in turning back to mediæval ways ; and like Leibniz, too, are those contemporary thinkers who, anxious to introduce Christian order and principle into industry and commerce, look back for guidance to the great attempt of the mediæval Church to Christianise economics. There is life and inspiration, as well as aridity and unreality, in the social theories of the Middle Ages. We are here confronted with what seems to be a contradiction; but we can solve that contradiction if we resolve not to cling too closely to the theories of mediæval writers, but to look at mediæval thought in all its length and breadth. After all, there is such a thing as political thought, which is distinct from, and greater than, political theory. Political theory is the speculation of particular thinkers, which may be remote from the actual facts of the time. Political thought is the immanent philosophy of a whole age, which determines its action and shapes its life. The one is explicit, self-conscious, and (it may be) detached : the other is implicit, unconscious, and immersed in the stream of vital action. There was abundant political thought in the Middle Ages, just because they were ages of formation and fermentation, in which the Christian leaven—the great new thing in the world—was steadily permeating society, and the fresh Germanic influx into the ancient world was finding its place and its level. Look at the Church, and you will see the clergy seeking, on the one hand, to formulate its relations with the temporal power, and, on the other, to inform with its own principles of peace and justice and godliness the feudal life of the country, the commercial life of the town, and the student life of the university. Look at feudalism, and you will see it giving to society the new cohesive force of the bond of personal loyalty, and the new conception that the landowner is in honour bound to render service, in war and in peace, to the community in which—we may almost say, from which—he holds his land. Look at the new structure of the three estates, and you will find it developing into that great gift of the Middle Ages to the modern world—the gift of representative institutions. Look at the communes and the guilds of the mediæval cities, and you will see the basis of a new economics and a new type of self-government. If you look at these things, and if you see these visions, you will realise that the Middle Ages lived, and lived abundantly. And anything which has lived, and lived abundantly, in the past, is still a part of the present—a root of its life ; an inspiration of its thought. The Middle Ages, therefore, are not dead. They live among us, and are contemporary with us, in many institutions of our life and many modes of our thought.

There are two periods in the Middle Ages, if we take them, as I propose that we should, to mean the great centuries that lie between the beginning of the Gregorian movement of the eleventh century and the beginning of the Protestant Reformation. There is the golden and . classical age, which ends with Boniface VIII—the age of the enthroned Papacy and the Church triumphant; the age of the great experiment of a Christian community controlled throughout by Christian principle. There is the silver and turbulent age of the fourteenth and fifteenth centuries, in which the Papacy is menaced by kings, by sects, and by councils; in which villeins revolt in the country and artizans are insurgent in towns; in which theory becomes radical, lay, and revolutionary. It is with the first of these periods that we shall be specially concerned.

The note of all mediæval thought is its universalism. It assumes the existence of a single universal society, which, on its lay side, is the inheritance and continuation of the ancient Roman Empire; and, on its ecclesiastical side, the incarnation of Christ in a visible Church. The same society—and this is an important matter, on which we shall have occasion to dwell again later—is thus at once an Empire and a Church. On the one side it has an Emperor, for things temporal; on the other it has a Pope, for things spiritual. The original theory of their relations, as it was formulated by Gelasius I at the end of the fifth century, was a theory of parallelism. Each had his sphere, and each abode in his sphere: the things that were Cæsar's were rendered to Cæsar, and the things that were Peter's to Peter. This scheme of mingled universalism and parallelism was disturbed by the barbaric invasions. Those invasions resulted in the rise of separate *regna*; and they also resulted in the rise of practically separate territorial churches—or, as the Germans call them, *Landeskirchen*—which fell largely under lay control. It was the work of Charlemagne to restore universalism, or at any rate a form of universalism, on the secular side : it was the work of Hildebrand to restore it also on the ecclesiastical side, by substituting a universal papal Church for the laicised territorial churches of previous centuries. But if universalism was thus restored, and restored on both its sides, the same was not true of parallelism. Hildebrand and his school had no wish for an Emperor who was an equal coadjutor of the Pope. They preferred a papal monarchy to a system of dyarchy.

The policy of the Hildebrandine school, and the politico-ecclesiastical thought which lies behind it, are of cardinal importance in mediæval thought. The key-note of that policy was *justitia*. *Justitia* meant, in the first place, the papal sovereignty over the Church. The Christ incarnate in a visible, historical, traditional Church must have His visible representative as the head of that Church on earth, the fountain of all ecclesiastical power, the exponent of all religious tradition. In the second place, *justitia* meant the liberation of the clergy from the lay world— from the social bond of matrimony, the economic bond of simony, and the feudal bond of lay investiture. In a sense, therefore, it meant the separation and the liberation of the Church from the State. But the separation of the Church from the State was not the separation of the State from the Church. The sovereign Pope might exclude the temporal power from things spiritual : he could not, being sovereign, exclude the spiritual power from things temporal. *Justitia*, therefore, meant, in the third place, the right of the Pope, as the sovereign exponent of the sovereign law of Christ, to judge and correct even kings and princes if they contravened that law or hindered its free operation. In principle, therefore (I quote the words from Tröltsch), " the State is subordinated to the Church, as an instrument under the control of the Church for the governance of temporal things, and for the bringing of temporal relations and values under the absolute spiritual purpose of which the hierarchy is guardian. The dogma of universal episcopacy involves for its completion the dogma of theocracy."

We may understand this position more clearly if we keep a firm hold of the notion of a single universal society. When we speak of Church and State in any consideration of the Middle Ages, we must remember that we are not speaking of two societies, but rather of the two governments of a single society. To-day in England Church and State are two societies; but they have one government, which is the king in Parliament. It was the opposite in the Middle Ages. Church and State were one society; but the one society had two governments. There might be, and there were, disputes between the two governments; but the society was and remained undivided. It was a single *Respublica Christiana*, in which churchmanship was coextensive with citizenship. You could not be a member of a political society unless you were a baptised Christian; and if you were excommunicated by the authorities of the Church you lost all legal and political rights. This was a mode of thought which survived the Middle Ages, and appeared in the Elizabethan system and the Clarendon Code. It is a mode of thought which really postulates a single sovereignty, even if it permits two governments. A single society must have, in the last resort, a single principle of life and a single sovereign exponent of that principle. The high papalist unitarians, who stood for papal sovereignty, had the best of the argument when they objected to the imperialist supporters of parallelism that *duo principia ponunt, quod est absurdum*. In the same way, and according to the same logic, it necessarily resulted, when the Reformation substituted a papal Cæsar for a Cæsarian Pope in England, that this papal Cæsar claimed governance alike in all causes, as well ecclesiastical as temporal.

The core of mediæval political thought, as it grew to maturity under the ripening influence of the Hildebrandine movement, is thus the conception of a single universal society, living under one principle of life, which is expounded in the last resort by a single authority. The principle is divine : the authority is a divine representative; that is why we may speak of a theocracy. The Church, enthroning itself over Christian society, makes a great and gallant attempt to unify all life, in all its reaches—political, social, economic, intellectual—under the control of Christian principle. Politically, it attempts to rebuke and correct kings for internal misgovernment, as when they falsify coinage, and for external misdoing, as when they break treaties ; socially, it controls the life of the family by the law of marriage which it administers, and the life of the individual by its system of penance ; economically, it seeks to regulate commerce and industry by enforcing just prices and prohibiting interest, as it seeks to control the economic motive in general by its conception of property as a trust held for the general benefit and by its inculcation of charity ; intellectually, it develops a single culture in the universities which are its organs, and in the last resort it enforces that culture by the persecution of heresy. It is a magnificent attempt at a synthesis of the whole of life by a sovereign wisdom. We can only realise how the attempt could be made, and carried so far with so much success, if we remember that the material on which it was made was much more simple, much more elementary, and

15

therefore much less intractable, than the material of our present life. There was no organised State to confront the clergy. It has often been said that in the Middle Ages there was no State; and at any rate we may say that— apart from England, which from the reign of Henry II rapidly developed a precocious State on a legal basis— there were only feudal communities, dissipated in fiefs and communes, with no regular officials or organised methods of action. Nor, again, was there any developed system of economics. Life ran on the basis of an economy in kind : money was scarce, and payments were made in labour or produce; agriculture was dominant; industry was an infant, ready to submit to discipline. Above all, there was a simple faith in the Church, as the depository of the means of salvation and the dispenser of those means through its holy sacraments, which made men ready to accept its sovereign wisdom humbly, meekly kneeling upon their knees. And this Church was an organised institution, with a system of officials, a body of law, and a sovereign pontiff able to control administration and interpret law.

We can hardly, therefore, speak of any politics or political theory in the Middle Ages as a separate or distinguishable factor or subject of study. Politics, economics, ethics, theology—all these run into one and are blended together; or, more strictly speaking, politics and economics are subordinated to ethics, which itself is revealed ethics, and therefore theology. Here—with the one and fundamental difference of revelation—the Middle Ages are like the ancient Greek world; and mediæval theory comes nearest to that of Plato. For in the ancient Greek world also politics and economics were subordinated to ethics; and in the thought of Plato ethics was in turn dependent, if not upon revelation, at any rate upon a system of meta-physics which had its analogies with mediæval theology. There is indeed a remarkable parallel between mediævalism and Platonism—the Platonism of the *Republic* and the *Laws*. For Plato too desires the control of all human life by a single wisdom, which for him is vested in the philosopher kings, as for the Middle Ages it was vested in the clergy—a control of the family and property, a control of culture and education, of music and poetry and drama. Do we not hear the Middle Ages speaking, when we read in Plato of the philosopher kings, how " one feature they will erase, and another they will put in, until they have made the ways of men, as far as possible, agreeable to the ways of God " ? [1] And what can be more mediæval than the system of persecution which Plato advocates in the *Laws* against all who deny the articles of his creed of natural religion ?

We have now to inquire into the nature of the principle by which the mediæval Church sought to direct the whole life of the Christian commonwealth. In Christian termino-logy, that principle was the revealed law of God. But the Church had inherited the culture of the ancient world ; and in that culture there was speech of a natural law—the law conformable to nature, about which the Stoics had theorised, and which the Roman lawyers had received into their legal system. We may say roughly (but only roughly : for in the handling of this matter, particularly in the writings of St Thomas, there are many refinements and distinctions) that the Church identified the divine law, as revealed to Moses and declared by our Lord, with the

---

[1] *Republic*, 501 *b,c*. On the parallels between Platonism and mediævalism see Zeller, *Vorträge und Abhandlungen*, vol. i ; Tröltsch, *Die Soziallehren der christlichen Kirchen*, pp. 182, 216, 233 ; and Barker, *Greek Political Theory*, pp. 210, 351, 352, 367-368, and specially pp. 383-386.

pure and undefiled principle of natural law. But here a difficulty arose. It was impossible to apply this law, at once divine and natural, to the control of human life and relations. In the purity of natural law there can be no government, for all men are free and equal ; for the same reason there can be no slavery ; nor, again, can there be any private property, for men who are free and equal hold all things in common. But in the actual world, government and slavery and private property existed ; nor could they be conjured away, whatever the strength of the Church or its desire to control human life according to the perfect law. The Church was accordingly forced to make an accommodation and to draw a distinction. In order to adjust its demands to what was possible, it established a difference between the absolute and the relative law of nature. The absolute law was the law as it stood before the fall : the relative law was the law as it stood after the fall. The law of nature after the fall was accommodated, and made relative, to the sinfulness which followed the fall. It became at once the penalty and the remedy of that sinfulness—the penalty, in the sense that it introduced the compulsion and the rigour of government and slavery and property ; the remedy, in the sense that it introduced the correction and the direction of sinfulness which are implied in these institutions. Private property, for example, is the penalty of sinfulness, in the sense that it abolishes the enjoyment of all things which existed before the fall ; but it is at the same time the remedy of sinfulness, in the sense that by permitting a limited satisfaction of the acquisitive passion it draws the worst of its sting. Thus the Church surrendered ; and yet it gained. It surrendered the absolute standard of freedom, equality, and communism ; it gained, on the

18

other hand, the opportunity of controlling Christian society, just because the relative standard which it adopted was capable of application to actual life.

Before we investigate further the features of this relative law of nature it is worth while to emphasise the conception of the sovereignty of law which it entailed. We believe in the sovereignty of law in England ; but we also believe in the sovereignty of Parliament, and our sovereign law is after all the subject of Parliament. The *lex* which was *rex* to mediæval thinkers was a law which did not proceed from a human legislature. So far as it was revealed, it was the stern daughter of the voice of God ; so far as it was natural, it was the inevitable outcome of the reason in man, whereby he discovers the mind of God. From either point of view, it was universal and eternal. It permeated all human society ; it knew no end of its validity. It followed that all human actions took place in a preexisting and all-determining atmosphere of law, and that they were valid when they conformed to its rules and invalid when they did not. " All custom," writes Gratian, " and all written law, which is adverse to natural law, is to be counted null and void." This law is thus the sovereign principle of human society. It limits kings and legislatures internally : it limits states in their relation to states externally. And of this law, because in one of its aspects it is the revelation and commandment of God, the Church is the custodian and exponent. We can readily see that so long as this idea of a law of nature identical with the law of God continues to be entertained, the Church will continue its attempt to control all human life in its light. We can see that on the strength of this law the Church can supervise Acts of Parliament, control guild ordinances, regulate the keeping of international

19

treaties, inspect the working of royal administration. For all these are under the law; and the Church has the knowledge of the law.[1]

The mediæval theory of the State—or rather of kingship, for the Middle Ages are a time of kings rather than of states—depends upon the conception of the relative law of nature. Kingship is a penalty for sin, and indeed, in so far as it satisfies the passion for domination, it is itself tainted with sin; but it is also a remedy for sin, since its object is the punishment of iniquity and the doing of justice, and as such it is divinely ordained. Sometimes the first of these objects may be emphasised, and kings may seem to appear as the devil's tools. " Who is there but knows," wrote Gregory VII in a famous passage, " that kings took their beginning from those who, ignorant of God . . . spurred by the Devil, who is the prince of this world, in blind passion and intolerable presumption sought to rule over their equals ? " More often, and more naturally (if one is thinking in terms of relative nature), it is the second aspect which receives recognition. We find this aspect emphasised not only in the theory, but also in the ritual, of the Church. The coronation ceremony, which begins to appear in the early Middle Ages, implies in itself a whole conception of kingship. It contains a form of election, nominally by human electors, but ultimately—since the Holy Spirit is conceived to descend on the electors—by God Himself. It contains a ceremony of anointing, whereby the king receives an unction which he may claim to be indelible, and is ordained, as it were, to a holy office and a divine right.

---

[1] It may be remarked that in England at any rate there was a conception that the king was subject to and limited by even positive law. Magna Carta means (Maitland has said) that the king is and shall be below the law. The notion of a fundamental positive law long persisted (see McIlwaine, *The High Court of Parliament*).

It contains a form of oath, by which the king is pledged in a triple pledge—to defend the Church, to repress rapine and iniquity, and to enjoin justice and mercy. By all these things—his election, his unction, his oath—he becomes an officer of the Church (*advocatus ecclesiæ*), bound to use his high powers for the purposes of the Church and the realisation of its sovereign principle of the relative law of nature.

Monarchy thus acquires a divine right; but just because it is divine it is limited. It must be exercised for the realisation of those absolute spiritual aims of which the Church is guardian : otherwise the Church will declare it forfeited, and proceed by excommunication to banish the king from Christian society, and therefore from the exercise of his right. Nor is this all. Divine right is in mediæval theory compatible and coexistent with popular institution. All power, it is true, proceeds from God, and is an emanation of His sovereignty, but the people have a voice in the institution of the person who wields royal power ; and by his oath at his coronation a king may be further conceived as having made a pact with his people to govern in a certain way. The people which has exercised a voice in the institution of a king may claim a voice in his deposition : the king who fails to fulfil his implied pact with his people ceases to deserve (says St Thomas) that the pact should be kept by his people. The popular basis and the popular right of criticism of monarchy are cardinal tenets of mediæval theory. St Thomas will even say that only the will of the people, or of the king as representing the people, can make a law. St Thomas—like the clerical thinkers of the Middle Ages in general—is a Whig ; he believes in popular sovereignty, popular institution of monarchy, a pact between king and people, and the general tenets of Locke. It was not idly that Sir Robert Filmer wrote that "this tenent was first hatched in the schools, and hath been fostered by all succeeding papists for good divinity." It is true that the schoolmen found the tenet in their texts. The Old Testament speaks of David making a covenant with his people; Roman Law, by the voice of Ulpian, ascribes the force of law to the will of the prince, because the people confers on him all its sovereignty and power; Aristotle, in a famous passage of the third book of the *Politics*, has something to say of the right of a multitude to elect its officials and also to call them to account. It is true again that it might be argued that even under the relative law of nature some traces of the freedom and equality of the absolute law must be preserved, and kings must still be kings of a free people even if equality were sacrificed. But it is also true that the tenet, whatever its grounds, was cheerfully embraced by the clergy of the Middle Ages because it suited their interests. Monarchy limited by the people was a powerful buttress to monarchy limited by the Church; and *libertas populi* and *libertas ecclesiæ* were good allies.

A political theory which reconciles divine right with a social contract may seem paradoxical to those who remember that divine right has been at daggers drawn with the social contract in modern history. But the reconciliation, however paradoxical it may seem, is an essential feature of mediæval thought. On the whole, the cause of liberalism, if we may use the word, had the chief advantage in the reconciliation. It is a limited kingship which emerges— a kingship limited by the law of nature, limited by the Church, limited by the people. There is thus no theorising about the sovereignty of the State in the Middle Ages;

but there is much theorising about the exact limits of its limited power. Mediæval theorists are almost like counsel arguing before a frontier commission : they seek to fix some frontier here or there, by this or that argument. It is, of course, the boundaries between kingship and priesthood which are most hotly in dispute. The counsel on one side advance the argument of parallelism : they proclaim the theory of equal but separate spheres, for the Emperor in things temporal and for the Pope in things spiritual. The argument, as we have seen, was first advanced by a Pope ; but in the high midday of the Middle Ages it was espoused by the imperialists, and found a magnificent exposition in Dante's treatise *On Monarchy*. The counsel on the other side advance the argument of unity : they hold that kingship is vested with the sword of justice by the priesthood, and is responsible to the priesthood for the manner of its exercise. We have already had occasion to remark that the counsel for unity have the better of the argument. We may add that it could not well have been otherwise under the actual conditions of the mediæval polity. The Pope was an acknowledged and absolute sovereign within the priesthood, supreme over bishops, supreme over all church courts, supreme over all the orders ; he had the *plenitudo potestatis* —and he knew what he had. Innocent IV has a clear conception of sovereignty : *optime omnium*, says Bodin, *jura majestatis novit*. The Emperor had only real power as German king ; and his power as German king was divided with feudatories innumerable. Compared with the Emperors, the Popes of the high Middle Ages were as iron pots clashing with earthen vessels. It is true that a change, and a great change, comes after 1300, in the evening of the Middle Ages. Of that change we must speak later. But we have already seen that the two periods of the Middle Ages—its noon and its evening—are very different.

It was common in mediæval theory to handle the problem of kingship in connexion with the problems of slavery and property. They were all methods of control, penalties and remedies for sin, founded on the relative law of nature. It may seem curious to find the thinkers of a Church based on the principles of Christ engaging in the defence of slavery. But they were aided by Aristotle ; and we have to remember that they belonged to an age in which prædial serfdom was universal and personal slavery still existed. Their treatment of the problem of property was more radical. It had been a general doctrine in the Church since the days of St Augustine that communism was the ideal condition of society ; and the great canonist Gratian is following tradition when he writes that " by the law of nature all things are the common property of all men—a principle followed by the primitive Church in Jerusalem, and taught by Plato." But this is a matter of the absolute law of nature ; and the canonists generally admit that as a result of sin private property is a necessary and useful institution, and is therefore justified by the relative law of nature. While they admit its necessity and its utility, however, they impose two limitations—the first, that a man can only be said to own that of which he makes a good use ; the second, that no man can take for himself more than he needs. In other words, private property must be justified by being used as an instrument for the realisation of a good will and for the good of the community ; nor must the claims of all to enjoy the use of such instruments be barred by their being accumulated in the hands of a few. By such principles private property

24

was at once recognised, as under the conditions of the age was necessary, and yet accommodated to Christian principle, as was equally necessary if the Church was to be true to its mission of Christianising human life. If charity abounded—if property were well distributed—then the Gospel, even if it was not entirely fulfilled, was not entirely set at nought. It was a compromise, an accommodation ; and in the fourteenth and fifteenth centuries, particularly among the Hussites, we shall find radical revolts against the compromise, and demands for a pure Christian communism. But the compromise had its value ; and it was at any rate the basis on which the Church could take its stand in seeking to enforce a system of just prices and to prohibit the taking of interest. For unjust prices and usury accumulate wealth in the hands of a few, and the profits they bring are apt to be hoarded rather than used for good.

There is one range of mediæval social practice which, while it did not greatly influence the explicit theory of the Middle Ages, is none the less one of the most important elements issuing from its general thought. This is the range of what we may call ' group-life,' which appears within the Church in the form of the various orders, and within the State in the form partly of local groups such as communes and guilds (not to mention shires or provinces), and partly of social groups such as estates. Within the Church group-life failed to attain any great measure of autonomy. It is true that the original Benedictine monasteries were each and all autonomous ; it is also true that the orders proper (for the Benedictines, not having a common government, were hardly orders) were centralised within themselves and centralised under the Papacy. The papal plenitude of power did not consort well with autonomous groups ; and Innocent IV, who knew so well the rights of sovereignty, knew also how to create and to use the conception of groups or corporations as nothing more than *fictæ personæ*, which it rested with the sovereign to create, control, and abrogate. It is within the much more amorphous State that group-life grows and spreads with a rich luxuriance during the Middle Ages. The State itself becomes a *communitas*, sown full of *communitates* ; nor shall we name it amiss if we call it a *communitas communitatum*—a federal group of groups.

Among these groups the town is not the least remarkable. As it grows to maturity, it becomes itself a group of groups ; for it embraces a number of guilds—each with its statutes and officials, its regular meetings and meeting-place—which need, and do not always readily find, co-ordination with one another and with the central civic community. The political thought implicit in the life of the rich and vigorous mediæval town (say Ghent, or Lübeck, or Florence) may almost be called more significant for modern life than the political thought implicit in that of the embryonic mediæval State. It is the town which attracts the special attention of St Thomas himself, for it is in the town that he sees the pattern of Christian society. In the country is feudalism ; and feudalism is a state of war, and a state in which possession bears no proportion to labour. The town is the home of peace, and a place in which a man receives according to what he has done. These are Christian ideals ; and the town is Christian in a still higher sense. " With its great cathedrals and its intense religious life " (once more I quote Tröltsch), " with its arts and guilds consecrated by religious observance, its social provision for spiritual

26

and temporal well-being, its Christian parish-schools and charitable institutions, its peace and its communal spirit, it is the zenith of the development of the mediæval spirit."

From our modern point of view, which leads us to concern ourselves with the problem of the part to be played by the organised occupation (guild, or trade union, or other association) in the scheme of our polity, the mediæval guilds have a fascination which needs no explanation. But there is another group—based, we may say, on the unorganised occupation, but none the less occupational in character—which also deserves our attention. This is the estate—the state or condition of men who follow a common calling and thus constitute a distinct class. The clergy, baronage, and commons—*oratores*, *bellatores*, and *laboratores*—form a three-class system which has its harbinger in Plato's *Republic*, and has left its traces in the English constitution. The development of Parliament and the growth of representative institutions are connected with this system. And when we reflect on the importance of these things in our modern system of representative government we must admit that mediæval political thought has added new cubits to our stature.

We have spoken of the groups, local and social, of which the State is composed : what shall we say of the conception of the State as itself a federal group of groups? Dr Gierke, in a famous work, has dwelt much on this conception. He has taught us that in the mediæval State groups came into existence of themselves, without any creation or ' fiction ' of the State, and that they acted by themselves, with little if any control from the State. Guilds grew into life ; and once they lived, they acted—they legislated and they did justice—as if it were a matter of inherent right. This is true enough; but it is a fact which ought to be closely connected with the amorphous character and the weak administration of the mediæval State. It abounded in groups, and in the practice of what we may call communal self-help, because it was not yet itself a fully organised group. When it became such it asserted itself and curtailed the rights of groups with no little vigour. We cannot argue from the position of groups in the mediæval State to the position of groups in the modern, just because the mediæval State is so different from the modern. The modern State has to make its own adjustment; and in that adjustment it would seem inevitable that groups should occupy a much less important place. The strong localism on which many mediæval groups depended has now disappeared before the growing centralisation which acceleration of transport has brought in its train. The social differences on which many other mediæval groups depended have equally disappeared before a growing equality. The new claimant to the position of an autonomous guild marks its modernity when it calls itself a ' national ' guild. But a national guild is perhaps incompatible with centralised nationalism. In a closely unified national State it is difficult to return to the Middle Ages, even on a new plane.

Some words must be said, by the way of epilogue, on those last two centuries of the Middle Ages—the fourteenth and the fifteenth—which are in so many ways different from the three previous centuries. To the period of an assured institutional Church, sitting in calm sovereignty, and regulating human life by a careful accommodation between ideal principle and actual tendency, there succeeds a period of sects and of revolution, a period of Spirituals and Lollards and Hussites, a period marked by a conciliar movement against papal sovereignty. To the period of an assured and static society, in which the nobility rose high and proud above dependents and serfs, there succeeded a period of villein risings in the country and turbulent movements of artisans in the towns. It is the day of sectarianism in the Church and of social democracy in lay society. All of us have heard of John Ball's famous couplet in England; there were similar doggerel verses in France:

> None is villein but the villain.
> If the gentry never gendered,
> All the world would be at peace.

While the institution of slavery, in the broader sense of that term, was thus challenged, the institution of private property, which had been justified by the same arguments, came also under criticism. Wycliffe, it is true, only attacked ecclesiastical property: when it came to the laity, he left even the unjust, who could plead no title, in occupation of their possessions—for " God must obey the Devil." The Taborites of Bohemia went further; they proclaimed the principle, " No mine and thine any more: private property is mortal sin." Thus sectarianism went hand in hand with what we should call socialism; and religious dissidence had its parallel in social revolt.

This was but natural. The orthodox Church, as we have seen, had made a compromise with the world and its institutions. Those who rebelled against the Church rebelled against the compromise; and those who rebelled against the compromise rebelled against the Church. The Church was instinct with the genius of Christianity; but the genius of Christianity was wider than the Church, and there were elements of our Lord's teaching—elements

29

of freedom, of equality, of abnegation of possessions, of poverty, of simplicity—which an institutional Church engaged in making a compromise with the world had necessarily obscured or omitted. These principles emerge in the sects ; and they emerge as a social dynamite. The relative law of nature is rejected : men seek the absolute law, or rather they seek the simple word of the Lord, which has come to them, and they base themselves strictly on the Bible. Roman law and Aristotle and even St Augustine fade : it is the day of the pure *lex evangelica*.

It is also the day in which the State begins to come by its own. The revolt against the Church was naturally the gain of the State ; and radicalism, though it might attack lordship and property, was not—at any rate in its results— inimical to kingship. The theory of the fourteenth century is anti-clerical and pro-State. These were the times of the Avignonese captivity, in which Germany and England both challenged a French Papacy. In the course of that challenge the theorists of the State vindicated for it an independent origin and an independent scope. They went even further ; they vindicated for it the right of correction of a delinquent Church. These developments are most patent in the theory of Marsilio. Following Aristotle, Marsilio declares the State natural—and natural not according to the relative law of nature, but purely and absolutely. He believes that the natural State is a commonwealth of free citizens ; he also believes that the true Church is the communion of the faithful. He has thus a democratic view of the State ; but more important is his democratic view of the Church, which practically eliminates Papacy and hierarchy. And if he applies a democratic view to both State and Church, it is for the State that he vindicates sovereignty. The final authority to which he would appeal in causes ecclesiastical is indeed a general council of the faithful or their representatives ; but it is to be summoned by the prince as the governing organ of the community. The clergy have no power of legislation or of jurisdiction : they are simply an organ of the community (*pars sacerdotalis*) devoted to purely religious functions : it is the community itself which legislates, and its other appointed organs which judge and execute judgment.

In the theory of Marsilio we may trace the return of the State. It is significant that he based his argument upon Aristotle, the philosopher of the secular πόλις. In some respects he is prophetic—prophetic of the Reformation, and even of Rousseau ; but on the whole he expounds his own age. It was the age of the death of a conception of human society (which had lasted during the thousand years since the Emperor Constantine) as primarily religious in its motive and interest, and essentially universal in its scope : it was the age of the birth of a lay State limited in its range to the nation. Boniface VIII had represented the old conception : Philippe le Bel had been the victorious champion of the new ; and it was in France that Marsilio had received his training. In such an age the old internationalism of the Middle Ages died, even if, in the moment of its death, it received its most splendid exposition in the *De Monarchia* of Dante. The Popes could no longer act as international arbitrators, or claim, as Innocent III had done, a cognisance of breaches of treaty-rights and of all offences against Christian peace : [1] kings went their own way, doing as seemed right in their eyes. The Emperors shrank to be kings of Bohemia ; we may hear the knell of the Middle Ages when we read in

[1] See Innocent's decretal *Novit.*

Bartolus of Sassoferrato that " each king is in his kingdom the emperor of his kingdom." Wycliffe is far more ecclesiastical in temper than Marsilio ; but even Wycliffe is the apostle of the divine right of kings. He had indeed no alternative : a rebel against the Papacy and the whole conception of an organised Church vested with a power of coercion over human life, he could not but become *pravus hæreticus, adhærens regali potestati.*

We may trace in the fourteenth century the rising of the streams which gather volume in the sixteenth. On the one hand there is a direct appeal to the Gospel, and an awakening of social radicalism in close connexion with this evangelical trend ; and these are continued in Protestantism and in the Peasants' Revolts which in Germany and England accompany the growth of Protestantism. On the other hand there is an exaltation of the State at the expense of the Church, and a vindication of its ' natural ' basis or ' divine ' commission ; and these again are continued in the sixteenth century, when kings and electors become *capita ecclesiæ* or *summi episcopi*, and Machiavelli and Bodin preach the majesty of the sovereign State. In the realm of political thought we may place the watershed between the Middle Ages and the modern world in the years which lie between the ending of the *De Monarchia* and the beginning of the *Defensor Pacis*. It is true that there are mediævalists even in the fifteenth century. Nicolas of Cusa was one, who, writing on ' Catholic Concordance,' might indeed argue, like Marsilio, for representative councils in the Church (and, for that matter, also in the Empire), but none the less believed in the essential mediæval idea of a single universal society which mirrored the harmony of Heaven. The stream of his thought never reached the open sea ; but it was

Henry VIII himself who had Marsilio's work translated into English, and sent to Oxford for Wycliffe's writings " wherewith to vex the Pope."

ERNEST BARKER

BIBLIOGRAPHY

This chapter is largely based on the section of E. Tröltsch's *Die Soziallehren der christlichen Kirchen*, which deals with the Middle Ages. See also O. Gierke, *Political Theories of the Middle Age*, in Maitland's translation; A. J. and R. W. Carlyle, *Mediæval Political Theory in the West*, vols. i–iv; J. N. Figgis, *Churches in the Modern State* (Appendix I, *Respublica Christiana*), *Divine Right of Kings*, ch. iii–iv, and *From Gerson to Grotius*, ch. i–ii; R. L. Poole, *Illustrations of the History of Mediæval Thought*; C. N. S. Woolf, *Bartolus of Sassoferrato*. It is hardly necessary to mention Bryce's *Holy Roman Empire*.

ST AUGUSTINE AND THE CITY OF GOD

I

ST AUGUSTINE (A.D. 354-430), the greatest of
the Fathers of the Latin Church, lived at one of
the most critical periods of the world's history. It
was the period during which Western Europe was passing
from the tutelage of the Roman Empire into the disorderly liberty of mediæval Christendom. At the time of
Augustine's birth the imperial power of the Cæsars
seemed to be re-establishing itself in virtue of the masterly
reorganisation of Diocletian and Constantine. When,
seventy-five years later, his long and laborious life drew
to a close, the vision of a revival of the Roman dominion
in the West had proved to be a mirage. The very city
in which he died, his African bishopric of Hippo, was at
the moment of his death beleaguered by a horde of savage
Vandals. The Roman frontiers had been broken, and
hosts of barbarians—Visigoths, Sueves, Alans, Burgun-
dians, Franks, and others—were pouring into Dacia,
Mœsia, Illyricum, Italy, Gaul, and Spain. Civilisation
and Catholicism alike appeared to be doomed. To
St Augustine, who was both a great Roman and a great
Christian, fell the tremendous task of interpreting to his
contemporaries the meaning of the awful catastrophe. He
had to explain the fall of the Empire whose dominion had.
been regarded as eternal. He had to portray the polity
of the future ; to depict the ideal toward which the Church
—which alone had spiritual power—should urge its way ;

34

to expose the foundations, and make clear the structure, of the City of God.

The fall of the Roman Empire in the West was the outstanding fact of the time. It is difficult for us—the heirs of so many subsequent ages—to realise the magnitude of the portent, as it appeared to men of that age, and particularly to members of the Christian Church. From the first the Church had been dominated by the Empire. Christ Himself had been born a Roman subject, had lived under the protection and restriction of Latin law, had suffered death at the mandate of an imperial official. The early apostles, and in particular St Paul, had found their evangelistic activities wholly conditioned by the institutions and ideas of the Roman administrative system; in the main, they concluded that the discipline of Rome prepared men for Christ, and that the justice of Rome was a defence against the fury of the unbelievers. Later, however, the government of the Cæsars developed hostility to the Christian community. The causes have often been canvassed and are not far to seek. The Cæsars instinctively perceived, and correctly judged, that the Empire as established by the craft of Augustus, and the Church as moulded by the imperial genius of St Paul, could not exist side by side. Each claimed a sovereignty which was fatal to the other. Hence the great persecutions of the Church by the State, and the great conspiracies against the State by the Church. The dualism became complete, and the furious conflict of the two rival authorities reached its climax in the half-century which began with the Emperor Decius and ended with the Emperor Diocletian (A.D. 250–304). The pagan State exerted all the power which it still possessed to crush the Christian Church out of existence.

35

It failed; and its failure was marked by the resignation of Diocletian and the conversion of his successor, Constantine. The Church and the Empire were reconciled. Three centuries of dualism were brought to an end. A *Respublica Christiana* was, in theory at least, set up—a Christian State in which the Emperor as *pontifex maximus* became *episcopus episcoporum*, and presided at œcumenical councils. The Church, filled with a sense of triumph and inspired by confident hope, supported by Cæsar and in grateful return exalting his prerogative, advanced to complete its capture of the State and its evangelisation of the world. It counted without misgiving upon the permanence of Rome and upon its own unbreakable unity.

Both the grounds of its assurance proved to be unsubstantial. On the one hand, the Empire no sooner had become Christian than it began to totter to its fall. On the other hand, the Church no sooner had attained to tranquillity than it began to be split in irremediable schism. To the Emperors, in all probability, the feature of the Church which had most impressed them had been that infrangible solidarity which had given it success in the face of the most ferocious assaults. The storms of controversy, the fires of persecution, the upheavals of mob-violence, all had assailed it in vain. It had stood, massive in its patient fortitude; a corporation stronger in the unity of its will, the singleness of its faith, the concentration of its loyalty, than the Empire itself. But with the removal of the external pressure of adversity that solidarity ceased. Differences of doctrine, particularly that which divided Arius from Athanasius, caused irreconcilable breaches; doubtful problems of discipline, particularly that associated with the Donatists, led to schismatical dissent; conflicts for office, emolument, property, power, distracted the episcopate, scandalised the faithful, and amazed the world. The Emperors, who, in the presence of external foes, above all things needed internal peace and unity, were profoundly disappointed and disgusted. As to doctrine, they did not mind what the bishops said, so long as they all said the same thing ; as to discipline, they were indifferent what rules the Church laid down, provided it acknowledged the supreme authority of the State ; as to property and power, they were willing richly to endow the episcopate, if only it would agree within itself as to the partition of the spoil. The Emperors, however, appealed in vain to the wrangling hierarchs. The Church victorious, instead of becoming, as had been hoped, a new source of strength and bond of union to the Empire, became a fresh cause of dissension, disintegration, and disaster. Constantine's son and successor signalised his disillusionment by proclaiming himself a heretic ; the next of the great Emperors of the fourth century, Julian, apostatised altogether.

Meantime, while controversy and confusion prevailed within the Empire, the threat of the barbarians beyond its river-frontiers became more and more insistent. An immense movement of the nations was in process, originating apparently in some gigantic upheaval among the nomadic hordes which occupied the pastoral table-lands of Central Asia. At length the Huns, expelled from their native steppes, made their way through that ancient gateway of wandering peoples which lies between the Ural Mountains and the Caspian Sea, and fell like a hurricane upon the already troubled West. The weakened barriers of the Roman dominion could no longer stand the strain. The Danube and the Rhine were crossed by barbarian invaders, and the Latin civilisation was threatened with submergence by floods of Teutonic savagery. First and most notable of these alien hosts were the Visigoths. Having crossed the Lower Danube in A.D. 376, and having defeated a great Roman army at Adrianople two years later, they were allowed to settle in the two provinces of Dacia and Mœsia (the northern regions of modern Serbia and Bulgaria). In A.D. 395, weary of peace and inactivity, they broke loose, and for nearly twenty years wandered and wasted, until they came to final rest in the valley of the Garonne. Macedonia, Thrace, Thessaly, Greece, Italy, Gaul, Spain, all experienced the horror of their depredations. But of all their deeds the one which caused the greatest stir in the world was the sack of the city of Rome in A.D. 410.

No city in the world had ever risen to such eminence as Rome. For eight centuries (since her capture by the Gauls in 390 B.C.) she had been inviolate. She had become the centre of the vastest and most powerful empire which had ever been established among mankind. The wealth of the world had been poured into her lap, and it had been used to adorn her with temples and palaces which were among the marvels of the earth. All roads led to her ; all men looked to her for guidance and control ; she was regarded as the symbol of all that was most potent and most enduring. True, she had suffered some loss of prestige and influence when Constantine (A.D. 330) built a ' New Rome ' on the Bosphorus, and made this Christian capital the seat of his government. But no imperial favour could transfer to the city of Constantine the loyalty and reverence which for many successive generations had gathered round the ancient city of the Seven Hills.

The departure of the Emperor ; his conversion to Christianity ; his founding of a new capital where churches and not temples had the places of prominence and honour ;

all these things tended to make Rome with its Senate the representative of the old order, and the place where the worship of the old gods was maintained in the greatest vigour. For eighty years (A.D. 313–393) Christianity and the Cults were allowed to live side by side in the Roman Empire. Then came, as the culmination of a long series of religious enactments increasingly favourable to the new faith, the edict of Theodosius I, totally prohibiting and proscribing the practice of paganism. Two years later, as we have seen, the ravages of the Visigoths began, reaching their climax in the sack of Rome itself (A.D. 410).

The sack of Rome caused almost equal consternation to pagans and to Christians. The devotees of the old gods—exasperated, humiliated, dispossessed, persecuted—raised aloud the cry," Rome has perished in the Christian days." They pointed to the victories which their fathers had won in the days when Jupiter, Neptune, Mars, and their fellows were venerated and served ; they enumerated the regions which had passed under Roman control through the divine favour of Cybele, Isis, Mithras, and the Syrian Baal ; they lauded the unity and strength which the Empire had derived from the worship of the spirit of the city and the genius of its prince ; they attributed all the calamities of their own dark days to the abandonment of the old faiths and to the consequent anger of the deserted and insulted deities. The Christians, for their part, though they repudiated the arguments of the pagans, were troubled to think that the conversion of the Empire had not sufficed to save it from this overwhelming and spectacular disaster, and were still more perturbed to realise that the imperial power in which they had trusted for temporal security and world-wide dominion, was unable to save even itself from destruction.

St Augustine heard both the cry of the pagans and the plaint of the Christians. He was in a position to understand each of them. The son of a pagan father and a Christian mother, he himself had passed from paganism— by the graded way of Manichæism, Scepticism, and Neo-Platonism—to the full confidence of Christian faith. Feeling the urgency of the problem to which the fall of Rome had given rise, he set himself to deal with it in all its aspects. The main appeal of the pagans had been to history. To history, then, he too would go. He set himself to survey—so far as his knowledge went, and his purpose required—the records of the human race. He made explicit what had been implicit in Christianity from the beginning, viz., a philosophy of history. He sought to interpret the course of mundane affairs, including the catastrophes of his own day, in terms of the eternal will of God. In his hands the story of mankind became a narrative of the unfolding in time and space of the eternal purpose of the Creator. He laid down the lines of that theodicy which, from the ampler stores of information afforded by later research, was developed by Bossuet in his *Discours sur l'histoire universelle*, by Vico in his *Nuova Scienza*, and by Schlegel in his *Philosophie der Geschichte*.

St Augustine began the writing of his *De Civitate Dei* in the year 413; it occupied him, with many intervals and much interruption, until 426. To this long and broken period of construction, with its distractions and discontinuities, is no doubt due the fact that it is one of the most difficult of books to read, that its definitions are vague and variable, that its argument is obscure, that its conclusions are still a subject of interminable controversy. Nevertheless, in spite of grave defects both in design and in execution, its grand idea is clear. It traces from the day of creation to the day of final judgment the history of the two societies whose conflict had been the outstanding feature of the four centuries of the Christian era. The one, the *Civitas Dei*, had its origin with the creation of the angels; the other, its rival, the *Civitas Terrena*, commenced with the fall of Satan. On earth, the one was founded by the pious Abel, the other by the impious Cain.

The story of these two societies is pursued in twenty-two books. These books fall into two main groups. Books 1–10 are defensive : they are concerned with rebutting the pagan charge, " Rome has perished in the Christian days." They show that the fate of Rome was not peculiar ; that earlier empires (in particular the Assyrian) had suffered extinction from causes other than Christian ; that Rome herself (*e.g.*, in 390 B.C.) had experienced calamities as great as that of A.D. 410, in days when the old gods were in the height of their ascendancy ; that, in general, the fall of earthly states could be adequately explained by, and indeed was directly attributable to, the vices which paganism bred—cruelty, extortion, pride, luxury, debauchery. They end by carrying the controversy into the pagan camp, and by contending that the catastrophe of 410 was mitigated, rather than caused, by the religion to whose authority the Gothic conquerors were constrained to render some obedience. Books 11–22 are constructive. They ask and answer the question, " If it is the fate of earthly dominion to pass away, is there a city which endures ? " Yes, replies Augustine, the city which shall have no end is that *Civitas Dei* which has its latest and most perfect terrestrial manifestation in the Christian Church. It is here, when Augustine touches the height of his great argument, and justifies the ways of God to men, that he becomes at once most magnificent and most obscure. What does Augustine mean by " the Church " ? Is it the visible and determinable Catholic community, or is it the invisible and indeterminable society of the predestined elect, known only to God ? It is impossible to be sure which of the two he has in mind. Again, what is the *Civitas Terrena* ? Is it the State, as such ? Is it to be identified in any way with the Roman Empire ? Here, also, it is hard to be certain what Augustine thought. Of this, however, there can be no doubt : Augustine was conscious that he was fighting a winning battle. He saw that the future of the world lay in the Christian Church, and he was confident that it would move on from triumph to triumph until the primal purpose of God was fulfilled.

THE EDITOR

II

My subject is the place of St Augustine in political theory. It must of course be recognised that St. Augustine is one of those great men who have left their mark upon various modes of thought for long ages, but how far his influence was real and significant in political thought is a matter which needs careful consideration.

In order to understand this question we must go back before St Augustine himself to an earlier period in Christian and in philosophical history. We must go back, in fact, behind the Christian conceptions of society and State to the conceptions of the post-Aristotelian philosophical thinkers, and especially to the conceptions of the Stoic writers. We have fortunately in one of the letters of Seneca a very complete account of the conceptions of the origins and the institutions of society which he derived, as he tells us, from Posidonius, one of the great masters of the Stoic School. In this statement of Seneca we find for the first time formally developed a conception of the origins of society and of the State which, as we shall see, is characteristic of the whole tradition of the Christian Fathers. Seneca conceives of the actual institution of the State as being conventional and not primitive. In the primitive world, as he believed, or at any rate as he represented it, men lived together in peace and in happiness, having all things in common ; there was no private property ; men were innocent and happy. There was order of the best kind, for men followed Nature. The best and wisest men were their rulers ; but they were rulers only in the sense that they guided and directed men for their good, and they were gladly obeyed, but there was no coercive order in the strict sense of the word. Seneca, indeed, did not regard this primitive condition as being one of perfection. It was, rather, a condition of innocence. It represented the undeveloped, not the developed, nature of man, but still, such as it was, it was a state of happiness, of at least negative virtue and goodness. As Seneca describes it, it is at least comparable with the traditions of the Golden Age as we find them in some of the earlier Greek poets.[1]

Whence it was that the Stoics derived these conceptions is indeed more than we can be said to know, but the significance of the conceptions is quite independent of our knowledge or ignorance of their source. They represent a mode of thought which has proved itself to be of immense importance in the history of political ideas, and one which, at least formally, governed European

[1] Seneca, *Epistles*, xiv, 2.

thought until toward the end of the eighteenth century. The State of nature in these Stoic writings is the same conception as that of Locke and of Rousseau's earlier work.

How then, we must ask, did it come about that men departed from this original state of innocence, and how did men pass into the conditions of the world such as we know them now ? The answer on the whole is clear and distinct ; men passed out of this state not through any instinct of progress, but through the appearance and development of vice. As Seneca says, their first innocence disappeared. Men became avaricious, dissatisfied with the common enjoyment of the good things of the world, and desired to hold them in their private possession. The wise, just, and kindly rulers of the primitive age gradually grew dissatisfied with the limitations of their paternal rule ; ambition seized upon them, and the kingship of the wise gave place to tyranny, so that men had to create laws which should control their rulers. Seneca, as you will observe, looks upon the institutions of society as being the result of vice, of the corruption of human nature. They are conventional institutions, made necessary by the actual defects of human nature rather than by the natural conditions of human progress. This is indeed the first form of what in later days has been sometimes called the police theory of the State ; namely, that the function of the State is not as the great Greek thinkers had conceived it, to help man's growth toward perfection, but rather that the organisation of the State is an unhappy necessity, the method of coercing and constraining the evil propensities of human nature.

It may at first sight seem rather strange to us that the political theory of the Stoics should be founded upon a conception so analogous to the traditional Christian conception of the fall of man, but such is the case. The Stoic theory does quite clearly conceive of a primitive catastrophe, out of which there have arisen not only the evils and misfortunes of human life, but also the various methods by which men endeavour to deal with these evils and difficulties. It is no doubt the coincidence of the Stoic theory with the traditional Christian theory which made it peculiarly easy for the Christian Fathers to accept the Stoic theory of the origin of the State and to adapt it to their own particular conceptions of human life. I would indeed myself venture to say that there is no reason to think that the Fathers had any characteristically Christian conception of the origins of society at all. I should myself say that it is much more likely that they simply accepted from the Stoics, from the post-Aristotelian philosophers, those principles which I have described, and adapted them to their own doctrinal conceptions. At any rate it is true that the theory which I have described as being set out by Seneca is the theory of all the Christian Fathers, as far as I know, without any exception. To make this clear to you I would refer you in the first place to a very important passage of St Irenæus, a great Christian writer of the latter part of the second century, in his great work against Heresies.[1] In this you will find that the cause which has made government necessary is that men departed from God and hated their fellow-men and fell into confusion and disorder of every kind, and it thus came about that God put men over each other, imposing the fear of man upon man, and subjecting men to the authority of men, that by this means they might be compelled to some measure of righteousness and just dealing. We have here an explicit statement that the institution of government

[1] *Adv. Hær.*, v, 24.

has been made necessary by sin, while it is also a divinely appointed remedy for sin.

It is in this connection, I think, that we can best understand the position of St Augustine. St Augustine, in the *De Civitate Dei*,[1] laid down emphatically the principle that God did not make the rational man, who was created in His image, to rule over his fellow-men, but only over the irrational animals, and thus the first men were called rather shepherds of their flocks than kings of men. But here we must be careful in the conclusions which we draw. We might imagine that St Irenæus and St Augustine are condemning the institutions of human society as being the results of sin. Their statements might be interpreted as meaning that these institutions are in their proper nature sinful. It is, indeed, perfectly true that they meant not merely that they arose out of sin, but that they do in some measure express desires and passions which remain sinful. But the institutions are not, properly speaking, sinful, but rather the remedy for sin. We must take careful account of this if we are to understand the position either of St Augustine, or of the other Christian Fathers, or of the Middle Ages. In one famous letter, which is doubtless familiar to my readers, Hildebrand (Gregory VII) denounced kingship as something which had its origin in human sin, in the evil desires and passions of the human heart,[2] and some who have not been cautious have drawn from this the entirely incorrect conclusion that Hildebrand meant that human government was in its nature sinful. But that is a misconception due to the fact that people have not asked themselves how it was that Hildebrand came to use these phrases. Irenæus, as I said, described coercive authority as arising from the fact

---

[1] xix, 15.   [2] Gregory VII, *Registrum*, viii, 21.

that men had departed from God, but at the same time he was quite clear that it is God who has set men over each other. It is God who has imposed the fear of man upon men, and God does this in order that men may be compelled to some measure of righteousness and just dealing. Indeed, Irenæus in the same passage asserts that the devil, who was always a liar, never lied more greatly than when in the temptation he said to our Lord that the kingdoms of the world were his, and that he could give them to whom he would. For it is not the devil at all who has the right to the kingdoms of the world, but God Himself; and Irenæus enforced this by references to the Holy Scriptures, and especially to that famous passage in which St Paul speaks of the political authority, " the powers that be," as ordained by God.

We must be careful, then, to observe that Irenæus and, with him, all the Fathers are perfectly clear that the institution of government is derived directly from the institution of God Himself. No doubt it is from the sinful passions of men that the ambition to possess authority arises ; but, on the other hand, God has used this sinful ambition which is in human nature to create some system of order and of discipline in society, by which the graver vices of men may be restrained, if they cannot be wholly eradicated. What is true of the Fathers in general is also true of St Augustine ; I do not think that he in any way intended to suggest that government or the general authority of one man over another was illegitimate, or in its nature sinful ; but only that in the original condition of man there was no such authority, because men were innocent, and that it was only under the actual conditions of human vice that such a system of disciplinary authority was necessary. It is clear that he regarded the institution of slavery from the same point of view. Slavery was the consequence of man's sin, but in St Augustine's view it was also a divine remedy for the sinful nature of man.

We have thus endeavoured to make clear to ourselves what it was that St Augustine in general terms thought about the nature of the political authority of the State, and, if I am right in the considerations which I have here put forward, there is so far no substantial difference between the mode of thought of St Augustine and that of St Paul and the Christian Fathers in general. It is at the same time, no doubt, extremely difficult to be quite certain as to what St Augustine's view was on all the aspects of this question. It is not indeed certain that he was always consistent with himself. It is, for example, obviously true, when we turn again to the treatise *De Civitate Dei*, that he is engaged in comparing and contrasting the nature of the heavenly or spiritual city with the conditions and circumstances of the temporal city, and there have been those who have tended to conclude that he looked upon the Church as the terrestrial representative of the City of God, while he looked upon the State as belonging to some different and alien order. But it is more than doubtful whether this position can be maintained. I have already said that it seems to be clear that he did not intend to repudiate the general doctrine of the Fathers as to the divine nature of the origin of the State, but only to correct certain misapprehensions about it. There is no doubt that he conceived of the Temporal Power as being inferior in dignity and in greatness to the Spiritual Power, but I do not think that he had very clearly before him what we call the questions of the relation of Church and State. These were not, I think, present to his mind at all in the same way or in the same sense as, for instance, they were to the mind of St Ambrose, and I do not think that it is safe to found upon the writings of St Augustine the conclusion that he would have looked upon the Church as having in its proper nature any kind of relation of authority or supremacy over the State.

There is, however, one aspect of the State in St Augustine which is plain and explicit and which we must consider a little more particularly. It is the question of the relation of the State to justice. As some of my readers will know, there is nothing which is more emphatically asserted by Cicero in his treatment of the nature of the State than the principle that it is founded upon justice. It may be remembered that in Cicero's treatise *De Republica* he gives with approval the definition of the State as not being any multitude of men, but a multitude of men united in their agreement upon Law (*jus*) and in the common enjoyment of that which is useful to them. St Augustine rightly recognised that Cicero meant that there could be no true State without justice, because where there is no justice there can be no *jus*. But St Augustine found it impossible to apply this definition to such a State as that of Rome, at least in pagan times. For, he objects, how can you speak of justice among men who do not serve God. There is no justice in men who do such things, and there can, therefore, be no justice in a society formed of such men.[1] This definition then, he argues, will not work, and he proceeds to search for some other definition which may make it possible to admit that Rome had been a true State. This is given in a later chapter of the same book of the City of God, and is as follows : " A people is a multitude joined together in the

---

[1] *De Civitate Dei*, xix, 21.

common enjoyment of the things which it loves." A political society, that is, may be more or less corrupt, but so long as it consists of a multitude of rational beings, associated together in the harmonious enjoyment of that which they love, St Augustine thinks it may be regarded as a true State or commonwealth.[1] Whether St Augustine realised the enormous significance of what he was saying may be doubted; this definition is indeed practically the definition of Cicero, but with the element of law and justice left out, and no more fundamental difference could very well be imagined, for Cicero's whole conception of the State turns upon this principle, that it is a means for attaining and for preserving justice.

Now I am by no means clear myself whether the phrases of St Augustine in this place represent a settled conviction or a merely casual and isolated judgment. Many of the other references which he makes to the State, while they correspond in some measure with this definition, are ambiguous, though they would seem to indicate a persistence in leaving out the moral or ethical conception of the nature of the State. If this omission of St Augustine's had really been carefully considered by him, and if it was deliberate and persistent, it would represent a conception of the nature of political society of the gravest significance, for it would mean that perhaps the most influential of all Christian teachers desired to eliminate the conception of justice from the theory of the nature of the State. And if this was deliberate and considered it would have meant the introduction into the world of a conception of the State which might have gravely modified the whole history of political ideas. It must, however, be recognised that it is at least doubtful whether St Augustine

[1] *De Civitate Dei*, xix, 24.

really meant what he seems to say. In another chapter of the *De Civitate Dei*, after discussing the advantages of living in peace and goodwill with one's neighbours, he draws out a comparison between a band of robbers and a kingdom, and seems to mean that the only point of distinction, but still the real point of distinction, is that the latter has the quality of justice.[1] I am myself, therefore, not at all certain whether St Augustine did deliberately attempt to change the conception of the State. If he did, I cannot but feel that it was a deplorable error for a great Christian teacher.

Happily the matter is not important, for if indeed he did make this mistake it had no significance in the history of Christian ideas. It is a notable fact that this passage of St Augustine is hardly ever quoted at all in later Christian writers. The *De Civitate Dei* is constantly appealed to in the Middle Ages, and Cicero's definitions of the State are constantly quoted from St Augustine by the mediæval writers. But his own attempt to eliminate the conception of justice from the notion of the State is passed over in silence, and I can only say, therefore, that, if it was intended and deliberate, it had no significance; it had no correspondence with the movements of the human thought of later times, at any rate until we come down to the great but eccentric and abnormal genius of Hobbes in the seventeenth century.

If then, finally, we endeavour to ask whether the theory of St Augustine with relation to the State had great importance either in his own time or in the Middle Ages, I think we must answer that so far as it was different from the normal traditions of the Stoic philosophers and of the Christian Fathers it had no importance and no

[1] iv, 4.

significance, but that so far as it corresponded with these, so far as in his own way and under his own terms he re-stated the traditional view of the Stoics and of the Christian Fathers, it may well be said that St Augustine had much influence.

A. J. CARLYLE

BIBLIOGRAPHY

A. PRIMARY SOURCES

Augustinus, Sanctus Aurelius : Opera Omnia. 11 vols. Paris, 1679–1700.
Augustinus, Sanctus Aurelius : De Civitate Dei. Ed. E. Hoffmann. 2 vols. Vienna, 1898.
DODS, MARCUS : *The City of God :* A Translation into English. 2 vols. Edinburgh, 1897.
HEALEY, JOHN : *The City of God :* A Translation into English. 2 vols. London, 1610.

B. SECONDARY SOURCES

ANGUS, S. : *The Sources of the First Ten Books of Augustine's City of God.* Princeton, 1906.
CUNNINGHAM, W. : *Saint Austin and his Place in the History of Christian Thought.* Cambridge, 1885.
DORNER, I. A. : *Augustinus.* Berlin, 1873.
FIGGIS, J. N. : *The Political Aspects of Saint Augustine's City of God.* London, 1921.
HERTLING, G. VON : *Augustin.* Mainz, 1902.
HUMPHREYS, E. : *Politics and Religion in the Days of Augustine.* Columbia University, 1912.
McCABE, J. : *Saint Augustine and his Age.* London, 1902.
MAUSBACH, J. : *Die Ethik des heiligen Augustinus.* Freiburg, 1909.
REUTER, A. : *Augustinische Studien.* Gotha, 1887.
SCHOLZ, H. : *Glaube und Unglaube in der Weltgeschichte.* Leipzig, 1911.
SEIDEL, B. : *Die Lehre des heiligen Augustinus vom Staate.* Berlin, 1909.
THOMAS, F. : *S. Augustin, La Cité de Dieu.* Geneva, 1886.
TRÖLTSCH, E. : *Augustin, die christliche Antike und die Mittelalter.* Berlin, 1915.

III

JOHN OF SALISBURY AND THE
POLICRATICUS

IT is an interesting fact, not always fully realised, that
one of the most characteristic expressions of mediæval
political theory came from an Englishman. His countrymen, while interested and often attracted by his life and
personality, on the whole have not concerned themselves
much with his philosophy, partly, perhaps, from lack of
really good and accurate editions of his work, partly, one
fears, from that attitude of mind which regards the work of
any ' schoolman ' as unliterary and indigestible. · But after
the appearance of Professor Webb's text of the *Policraticus*,
with its admirable notes and glossaries, there has been little
excuse for their aloofness; and when the same editor gives
us the *Metalogicus* there will be less excuse still. Dr Poole
in his various studies has laid the foundation; and work is
urgently needed to supplement the critical contributions
of Prantl in his *History of Logic in the West* and of Schaarschmidt and Gennrich. The labour will be well repaid,
for it will bring the student into touch with one whom not
even the most ruthless of historical text-books (to which
we owe much of our aversion from mediæval philosophy)
could call a complete ' schoolman ' or condemn for aridity.
Nearly eight centuries divide John of Salisbury from
St Augustine ; and as we move forward through them we
shall be conscious of the great gap between the two epochs
and the profound contrast between the two personalities.

St Augustine stands on the confines of two worlds, embodies more than anyone else, as Mr Edwyn Bevan has expressed it, the transition from the classical world about to pass away to the world of Christendom.[1] John of Salisbury, on the other hand, is firmly set in the mediæval Christian polity, and belongs to its most confident and creative period. From the wreck of the Roman Empire the young *regna*—the separate kingdoms—have emerged. Everywhere there is promise of rich and abundant life—in the reformed and strengthened Papacy, in the universities where the scholastic movement had not long since begun, in the Norman states with their peaceful and ordered institutions, in the communes of Lombardy which were realising the interest and excitement of life in the Greek city-state once again. We have been transported into a European community, the members of which are held together by a common faith, by similarity of institutions, by the commerce of learning and scholarship, and it is to this that John of Salisbury belongs. The atmosphere of security makes itself felt in the very opening of his book. He writes no work of stern apologetic. When he starts his *Policraticus* he begins with an *Entheticus* (the very word is redolent of a comfortable library) of two hundred elegiac couplets of fairly graceful Latin, in the course of which he will play with the quantity of the *o* in *Britones* [2] or bring in fables from natural history [3]—what a contrast to the splendid and sonorous prose of St Augustine's dedication of the *De Civitate Dei* to Marcellinus, where he announced his intention to *defend* the most glorious City of God against

---

[1] *Hellenism and Christianity*, p. 142.
[2] *Entheticus*, in *Policraticus*, ed. C. C. J. Webb, p. 382 *b*. References throughout are to Professor Webb's text (Clarendon Press, 1909), the marginal pagination being adopted.
[3] *Ibid.*, p. 383 *a*.

all who preferred their own gods to its Founder ! But in the twelfth century Western Christianity was secure, and John was not engaged in defending what all accepted. Then again, immeasurably as St Augustine's influence had permeated Western theology, authoritative as his view of the relation between spiritual and temporal powers may have been, the twelfth-century disciple does not merely build on his fourth-century master's foundations or develop what had been begun either by him or by St Ambrose. Both St Augustine and John of Salisbury make the State serve the Church; but they reach their conclusion in different ways. St Augustine had said that it was the business of the State to secure peace in order that the spiritual power could maintain that justice which the secular power could not of itself practise. As against this limited aim of " peace," John of Salisbury, more positively, affirms " security of life " (*incolumitas vitæ*) to be the end of the State and defines it as " the perception of truth and the practice of virtue "; this—a moral end—the State may and can attain when organised and directed by the highest equity (*summæ æquitatis nutu*), and the key to its attainment is the union in closest co-ordination of the spiritual and temporal powers. Instead of adopting what is commonly known as the Gelasian theory of the separation of the two powers, which a political pessimism like that of St Augustine logically involves, John tends to advocate their close co-operation, the spiritual being compared to the soul of the body politic, the temporal to the head. For the earlier separation, then, is substituted the theory that there are two co-ordinate powers in the one organic *respublica* or commonwealth, whether that commonwealth be the totality of existing communities of Christendom (macrocosm) or one particular part or community of the whole

55

(microcosm).[1] I do not wish to anticipate a later discussion, but this point at the outset should be emphasised in order to show the great step forward which political thought is making.

So much for the contrast. In one respect, more obvious still, it might be prolonged. As we read John of Salisbury's work we shall doubt that the author ever felt St Augustine's travail of soul, ever went through an experience such as moved the great Father to reject as vain the art and the beauty he had admired and praised,[2] or was ever capable of the swift insight into the " abyss of human conscience " revealed in the *Confessions*. John is of a different nature ; he has clarity rather than intensity of vision, and it is what we should expect from his education and manner of life. Signor de Ruggiero has happily termed him " un gia moderno gentiluomo inglese, statistà, diplomatico, amatore eclettico di belle lettere," [3] though the description perhaps undervalues John's solid scholarship. These are attributes very natural in a member of the little society of learned men gathered at Archbishop Theobald's court, the place so charmingly described by Peter of Blois as " a camp of God, none other than the house of God and the gate of Heaven " ; [4] where were to be found scholars, lawyers, and administrators, who would

[1] P. Gennrich, *Die Staats- und Kirchenlehre Johanns von Salisbury*, p. 125 *et seq. Cf.* especially p. 129 : " Mit einem Worte : bei Augustin stehen Kirche und Staat begrifflich getrennt einander gegenüber ; Johann sucht beide zu einer Einheit zu verschmelzen, indem auch die Kirche in den Staat als den umfassenderen Organismus, freilich als dessen Seele und leitendes Prinzip eingegliedert wird. Es ist die Idee des universalen Menschheitsverbandes, welche die mittelalterliche Gesellschaftslehre beherrscht, die Johann zuerst im grossen wissenschaftlich durchzuführen versucht hat." Elsewhere (p. 4) in a fine phrase he describes John's conception of the State as that of " ein lebendiger Organismus der Gerechtigkeit."

[2] The change comes in the *Retractationes.*

[3] *Filosofia del Christianesimo,* ii, 247.

[4] Petrus Blessensis, *Ep.,* vi, in Migne, *Patrologia Latina,* ccvii, p. 18. *Cf.* the delightful picture of contemporary learned society in Stubbs, *Lectures on Mediæval and Modern History,* Nos. VI, VII.

openly discuss questions of public policy along with the problems of the schools. His life in the years before his chief works were published John has revealed to us in the autobiographical notes scattered up and down his chief works and his correspondence, while his friend Peter de la Celle has shown in his letters the sort of friendship John could inspire.[1] We see him acting in two principal capacities. He is the insatiable scholar who at about the age of twenty set out upon a ten years' course of study,[2] getting his teaching in dialectic from Abailard, Gilbert de la Porrée, and Robert of Melun, in composition and classical literature from the great teachers of Chartres, William of Conches and Richard L'Evêque,[3] and in rhetoric from Peter Helias ; so that the sombre Victorine theology which he would imbibe at Paris was tempered in him by the width and humanism of a great part of his training. Matured by study and travel, " beyond dispute," as Dr Poole has remarked, " the best-read man of his time," [4] he has become, now that his pupil and teaching days are over, secretary to Archbishop Theobald ; a great conductor of official correspondence, in frequent and friendly communication with the Chancellor, Thomas Becket ; constantly employed in the administrative routine of the Archbishop's court and in negotiations with the Curia, an expert on canon law procedure whom no Pope would ever have reproved for drinking deeply of English beer ; the friend (and very candid friend) of Adrian IV, whom long ago

---

[1] Petrus Cellensis, *Ep.*, lxix, in Migne, *P.L.*, ccii, p. 515, calls him " pars magna deliciarum mearum."

[2] If we accept Schaarschmidt's emendation *decennium* for *duodecennium* and reckon John's student life to have extended roughly from 1136 to 1145, as R. L. Poole in *Dict. Nat. Biog.*, xxix, 440.

[3] Probably not from Bernard of Chartres, as has been sometimes held. See R. L. Poole, " The Masters of the Schools at Paris and Chartres in John of Salisbury's Time," *Eng. Hist. Rev.*, xxxv, 321 *et seq.*

[4] *Illustrations of the History of Mediaeval Thought and Learning*, 1st ed., p. 219.

he may have known as 'Nick,' and an Englishman who knew his Rome as few of our countrymen in the Middle Ages knew it. Much of this experience of life and letters gained up to the year 1159 went into his two principal works, the *Policraticus* and the *Metalogicus*, which, by their mixture of personal reminiscences, satire, lecture-note material, current controversy, and fundamental religious conviction, open the gateway to the intellectual history of the twelfth century.

The *Policraticus* contains the bulk of his political thought and is his most influential work. The curious name, best translated *The Statesman's Book*, exhibits the typical and pathetic desire of the twelfth-century scholar who knew no Greek to find a Greek-sounding title for his work. It is also called *On the Vanities of Courtiers and the Footsteps of the Philosophers*: a strange mixture of two scarcely compatible elements, but we shall see how they are combined. The book is dedicated to the Chancellor, Thomas Becket, probably for two reasons: dedication to one so predominant at court as Becket would take the smart out of the more pointed satire aimed therein at the people at court,[1] and would be a pretty compliment wherewith to reinforce the more serious request for the King's pardon which both the author [2] and his master the Archbishop, on his behalf,[3] had made. For John had been getting into trouble with Henry II for denouncing, during the siege of Toulouse, the exactions levied upon the clergy to meet the cost of the expedition. To the Chancellor,

---

[1] *Pol.*, i, 387 *a* : " Et quia ne lædant aliquem, eum oportuit conveniri in quo nihil nugatorium possit argui, te virorum nostræ ætatis elegantissimum decrevi convenire, et quæ videnda in mei similibus arguenda describere."

[2] *Ep.*, cxiii.

[3] *Ep.*, lxiv, following Dr Poole, who (*Dict. Nat. Biog.*, loc. cit.) inclines to think this letter was written by Archbishop Theobald on John's behalf.

therefore, he has recourse for the material assurance of the King's pardon, to philosophy and letters he resorts for spiritual and abiding comfort. ✳Temporarily in disgrace, with plenty of enforced leisure, he has had time to think about the levity and stupidity which disfigure healthy political society, and has felt a strong reaction against the unnecessary elements which choke sound secular institutions.[1] For him philosophy serves to heighten the contrast between essentials and non-essentials, for the pursuit of truth is in some degree a process of elimination. It is the business of political theory, just as much as of dialectic in its sphere, to clear away the obstacles, and the clearing-away serves a useful purpose. In it the reader may recognise his own weaknesses and failings and call to mind the little saying, " Change the names and the story is about yourself." [2] " I may appear rather biting," John remarks, "but I have said what I have about our people [*nostratibus*] that they may return to the path of virtue, all unwilling though they be." [3] To discuss *quid maxime noceat fortunatis* and *quid in studiis alienum* has, therefore, its end. And it serves another purpose too. Big books, like lectures, need a little gaiety to make them acceptable, especially when they are concerned with morals or metaphysics. As John himself says, addressing his book :

> Sic igitur nugas sparges, ne tædia gignant
> Quæ rebus lætis sunt inimica nimis.
> Si iubet ut nugas agites, nugare decenter ;
> Nam sibi per nugas seria credet agi.[4]

---

[1] *Pol.*, i, 386 *b* : " Ego enim contempno quæ illi aulici ambiunt, et quæ ego ambio illi contempnunt. . . . Iam enim annis fere duodecim nugatum esse tædet et penitet me longe aliter institutum ; et quasi sacratioris philosophiæ lactatum uberibus ablactatumque decuerat ad philosophantium transisse cetum quam ad collegia nugatorum."

[2] i, 387 *a*.

[3] vi, 588 *d*.

[4] *Entheticus*, in *Pol.*, 381 *a*.

And John's playfulness, as he clears away the unnecessary things in the way of good, serious government, is diverting to read. Devoting his first three books to the removal of obstacles, he first chastises hunting and hunters from the Thebans (who first popularised the sport) and Nimrod, *robustus venator contra Dominum*, downward to modern times, and compares its devotees to centaurs, among whom you will find "seldom a modest or serious, seldom a self-controlled, never, I believe, a sober one."[1] Dicing, the more licentious forms of music, acting and conjuring, augury and interpretation of dreams when reduced to a science, astrology and astrological mathematics (termed *mathesis reprobata*), he would banish with Platonic rigour.

About the question of omens he is greatly exercised. Is the ruler of the State to pay heed to the so-called signs and portents which had such an influence on policy in classical times, or are all natural phenomena interpreted as such mere trifles, not to be regarded? His conclusions are strikingly free from the superstition of which the mediæval mind is sometimes accused. Natural phenomena, he thinks, do not bear rigid interpretations. They can be neither "good" nor "bad"—that is, favourable or the reverse. Their interpretation must depend on the general principle that nothing exists or happens that is not preceded by "legitimate cause and reason,"[2] and on the particular attitude of the beholder's mind. "The scientific man [*sapiens*] will turn whatever is said and done to his use and find therein material for the practice of virtue."[3] Interpretation that serves this practical purpose is very different from superstitious conjecture, and *con-*

---

[1] *Pol.*, i, 394 *a*.

[2] ii, 415 *d* : "Nichil enim est vel fit cuius ortum legitima causa et ratio non præcedant ; et, ut alius ait, nichil fit in terra sine causa."

[3] ii, 415 *a* : "Omnia cedunt in usum sapientis, habentque materiam virtutis exercendæ, quæcunque dicuntur aut fiunt."

jectoria is what John proceeds to chastise. In the same critical spirit he deals with flattery and flatterers, perhaps the most dangerous obstacle of all. As he continues, he is aware of the unpopularity which the satire of the first three books may bring upon his head; but he cannot forbear. Obeying the divine command that man should love man, he feels that he would be an unworthy disciple of his Master if he did not rejoice in all that is true and blaze with indignation against the enemies of the public weal.[1] But the 'blazing' is rendered acceptable by his sanity, common sense, and the happy erudition which can use Aulus Gellius, Persius, or Petronius equally with the Old Testament when illustrations to his points are required.[2]

The obstacles removed, he can come to more constructive work, the theory of political society for which he is chiefly known. The foundations are individualistic, and it may seem a little surprising that he is able to develop from what might appear to be a philosophy of asceticism a social theory of such importance. But herein he provides a good illustration of the peculiarly unempirical or deductive quality of mediæval political theory. To put the matter briefly, where we shall at first find difficulty in following him is in the transition from his individual to his social ethic. He assumes that the good of the community is assured by the virtue of all the individual members, that if each labour for his own salvation the common "safety" or weal (*salus publica*) is secure.[3] The

---

[1] iii, 477 *a*: "Hostis multorum fio dum ineptias nugatorum excutio." *Ibid.*, p. 477 *b*: "Unde patet indignum esse tanto magistro discipulum qui veritati non congaudet et adversus publicæ salutis hostes non excandescit."

[2] John's use of the classics is particularly noticed by Dr Poole, *Illustrations of Mediæval Thought and Learning*, 2nd ed., p. 123.

[3] *Pol.*, vi, 634 *a*: "Si enim in sui ipsius cultu quisque laboret et quæ exteriora sunt reputet aliena, profecto optimus erit status singulorum et omnium." *Cf.* Gennrich, *op. cit.*, p. 14.

salus publica must follow from the *salus singulorum et omnium*; it is, in fact, the safety or weal of the individual "writ large."[1]   If all the individuals are good, then the Whole must be good and in a state of security—here speaks Abailard's disciple.   Everything therefore depends on the meaning which John attaches to *salus*, and his explanation of the meaning of this word is characteristic in its theological colouring.   It is perception (or recognition [2]) of truth and the practice of virtue, and " truth " is, needless to say, God.   The reception of God into, and the indwelling of God in, the soul is the essential condition of virtuous activity ; and the community can only be " secure " when God has pervaded the soul of its every member, dwells ´in all His creatures alike, and is consciously recognised as

> A motion and a spirit, that impels
> All thinking things, all objects of all thought,
> And rolls through all things.[3]

In the first three books we shall look in vain for anything less apparently self-regarding in the term "security." The theory developed, based on Neo-Platonic doctrines of the soul and St Augustine's conception of grace, is intensely concerned with the individual.   True happiness (*vera beatitudo*) is the aim of every rational being.   What then is happiness ?   It is security of life (*incolumitas vitæ*) and consists in the perception of truth and the practice of

---

[1] iii, 479 *b* : " Agnitio igitur veritatis cultusque virtutis publica singulorum et omnium et rationalis naturæ universalis incolumitas est." iii, 477 *c* : " Est igitur salus publica, *quæ universos fovet et singulos*, incolumitas vitæ."

[2] "Agnitio veritatis." *Agnitio* is like the patristic ἐπίγνωσις, implying the recognition of something well known in the past, which has been temporarily obscured or forgotten.

[3] Wordsworth, "Lines composed a few miles above Tintern Abbey." *Cf. Pol.*, v, 542 *c* : "Est itaque nunc quasi singula in singulis, futurus, ut scriptum est, omnia in omnibus electis."

virtue. It is a condition only attained when God pervades the soul.[1] Now in the material world the soul cannot find true satisfaction ; for, unlike bodies that occupy space and so have a limit set to their extension, the soul has no such limit. The whole world is too small for its expansion. It can find satisfaction only when the living power of God fills it,[2] for God is the life of the soul.[3] How then is the soul to receive God? While the living power of God animates the whole creation, while everything that exists is what it is through participation in the life of God, while man has an innate desire (*appetitus*) to know the truth and to practise virtue, sin stands in the way.[4] Only through grace can God dwell in the souls of his reasonable creatures, and grace can come only through the love of God which drives out self-love, and through that knowledge of self which philosophy brings. Such a foundation of mystical thought would lead us to expect that to John of Salisbury the ideal organisation of society would be that of an ascetic community, each member of which spent his whole time examining his conscience and labouring for his salvation. For the fundamental basis of morality for John was the personal converse of the individual with God. The experience of that converse dominated everything.

[1] William of Conches' influence upon John may be considerable here. An interesting fragment of his teaching on the soul is given in Victor Cousin, *Fragments philosophiques*, pp. 394, 395. The twelfth-century commentary on the *Timæus* (*op. cit.*, p. 357) may also be his work, and, if so, help to explain certain passages in the *Policraticus*.

[2] *Pol.*, vii, 674 c. In the beautiful sentence " Maior enim est hiatus mentis quam corporis ; et, nisi seipsum Deus infundat, omnino nequit impleri."

[3] iii, 477 c, where is quoted the couplet :

" Vita animæ Deus est, hæc corporis ; hac fugiente
Solvitur hoc, perit hæc destituente Deo."

[4] iii, 478 c : " Sed cum sit in omnibus per naturam, sola inhabitat rationalia per gratiam." For the " innate desire " cf. *Metalogicus*, iv, c. 29 : " Appetitus enim hic naturaliter a Deo insitus est homini, etsi per naturam sine gratia perficere non potest."

But John's ideal State is not a community of monks,[1] and, for a while, he drops the asceticism. Some phrases which he used at the beginning of the third book [2] in describing the rule of the soul over the body evidently suggested to him the definition of the State which he was to explain in famous detail. Following the work which he knew as the *Institutio Traiani* and incorrectly attributed to Plutarch, he declares that the State or commonwealth (*respublica*) is a body animated by the benefit of the divine gift, conducted at the bidding of the highest equity and controlled by the rule of reason.[3] Mediæval thought, Dr Gierke has told us, proceeded from the idea of a single whole ; " under the influence of biblical allegories and the models set by Greek and Roman writers, the comparison of mankind at large and every smaller group to an animate body was universally adopted and pressed."[4] There is little need to reinforce the point by examples, a number of which are given in Dr Gierke's notes.[5] But it is John of Salisbury who first attempts to apply and work out the comparison in detail. In doing so he is led to the conclusion that a well-ordered constitution consists in the due allotment of functions to the members of the commonwealth and in the right condition, strength, and composition of each and every functionary body. There must be

---

[1] In *Pol.*, viii, 695 *d*, he praises the life of the cloister: " Nulla vita fidelior, nulla simplicior, nulla felicior quam eorum qui in claustris humiliter degunt." The monks " quasi terrestres angeli sunt totius mundanæ perturbationis ignari " (696 *a*).

[2] iii, 477 *d*.

[3] v, 540 *a*.

[4] *Political Theories of the Middle Age*, p. 25.

[5] *Ibid.*, notes 72–76 on pp. 130, 131. Professor Webb (note on *Pol.*, v, 540 *a*) also instances Abailard, *Epitome Theologiæ Christianæ*, c. 29 : " Unde et Apostolus Ecclesiam quasi quoddam animæ describit habens caput suum, ipsum scilicet Christum, oculos spiritales prælatos qui aliis præsident, manus ipsos operatores, pedes ipsos minores qui ad corpus portandum necessarii sunt."

mutual support among the members, and the closest
touch between them and their head ; in his literal words,
true *coherentia capitis et membrorum rei publicæ*, that the
unity of the body (which is the State) may be preserved.
The 'idea of organisation' is therefore dominant in
John's pages. The State he is describing is a functional
State, not altogether unlike Plato's, and the aim of each
part must be to do its own job, τὸ ἑαυτοῦ πράττειν.
This method, it will be clearly seen, precludes any discussion as to whether monarchy, oligarchy, or democracy,
or any admixture of them, is the best form of constitution.
John is no scientific student of constitutions, and the
universal prevalence of feudal institutions in the Europe
of his day did not provide him with much material for
a comparative study. He proceeds to develop the metaphor of the body. In the body the head and all the
members are guided by the soul. The soul's special task
is to love and reverence God. That love must be shown
by acts of worship, and worship may be of two kinds—the
mystic's contemplation and the enacted rite.[1] Though
pure contemplative adoration is the highest form of
reverence, God gave senses to man, and through the senses
He would be worshipped, through the body be served.[2]
This practical service falls to the task of a certain class or
order of men who are intermediaries between man and
God, and fulfil the part of the soul.[3] They are the clergy,
and to them as God's ministers and representatives—

---

[1] v, 542 *b* : " Colitur ergo Deus aut affectu mentis aut exhibitione operis."
[2] v, 544 *a* : " Sensualiter coli voluit qui sensum dedit."
[3] v, 543 *d* : " Ille autem cultus qui in exterioris operis exhibitione consistit,
medio indiget, eo quod ad spiritum corporalis nobis non patet accessus."
v, 540 *b* : " Ea vero quæ cultum religionis in nobis instituunt et Dei . . .
cerimonias tradunt, vicem animæ in corpore rei publicæ obtinent. Illos
vero, qui religionis cultui præsunt, quasi animam corporis suspicere et
venerari oportet. Quis enim sanctitatis ministros Dei ipsius vicarios esse
ambigit ? "

where John calls them His "friends"—the highest reverence must be shown. As divine law transcends human law, so those who minister in divine things are superior to those who minister in earthly things. "As the soul rules the body, so those whom he [the pseudo-Plutarch] calls the heads of religion in the State are set over the whole body." Their persons together with their places and instruments of worship are sacrosanct, and any form of sacrilege against them justly incurs excommunication which no force nor deceit can set aside.[1] The first lesson which the author whom he quotes was trying to inculcate into the prince was reverence and worship of God, and John follows his lead in putting this first among the duties of the ruler.[2]

If the soul is the clergy the head is the prince. As the soul rules the head and the rest of the body, it follows that he is subject to God and to those who hold His place on earth. This is emphasised in his election, in which divine, clerical, and popular elements concur. "Him," says our author, "the divine disposing has placed on the summit of the State," and "the secret mystery of His providence," the "judgment of His priests," and "the approbation of the whole people" have combined to put him there. John quotes the election of Joshua as leader of Israel as an instance of the people having a say in the choice: "Thus in the Old Testament we read that Moses, when about to ordain the man who was to be leader among the people, convoked the whole synagogue that he might be elected in their presence, lest afterwards any man might deny his authority

---

[1] v, 548 b: " Huius criminis alibi frustra quæritur venia, nisi articulus mortis forte immineat, quia nec per vim extorqueri nec surripi potest per fraudem."

[2] v, 541 b: " In summa ergo quattuor sunt quæ nititur rei publicæ principibus inculcare : reverentiam Dei, cultum sui, disciplinam officialium et potestatum, affectum et protectionem subditorum."

or any scruple be felt." Moses was further bidden to lay hands on him, to set him before Eleazar the priest, to give him a charge in the sight of the whole synagogue and to bestow his own honour upon him that the people might be obedient.[1] Every stage in this "election" John finds highly symbolical; and it is not a little interesting to find him applying to the election of the head of his State the principle applied by reforming clerical opinion to the election of bishops in the tenth and eleventh centuries, namely, that the bishop must be elected by the clergy and the people of his diocese.[2] Holding as he does such a theory of the prince's "election," his own particular way of stating the famous and inevitable doctrine of the two swords, though almost unique, does not come as a complete surprise. He declares that it was from the Church that the prince received the material sword as the minister of the priesthood, in order to be able to discharge that part of the priest's office which the spiritual power could not worthily exercise. Thus his conclusion is that the prince is the servant or "minister" of the priesthood and inferior to it because of his material function.[3]

Such views of the relation between soul and body, of the superiority of spiritual over temporal power, of the essential part played by the priesthood in the choice and ordination of the prince, are thoroughly in keeping with the characteristic and influential conception of the

---

[1] v, 549 a.

[2] Note particularly the canon promulgated at the Council of Rheims in 1049, that no one should be advanced to a post of command in the Church without election by clergy and people, and the judgment of the Council of Mainz the same year, which decided between the candidates for the Archbishopric of Besançon. A. J. Carlyle, *Mediæval Political Theory in the West*, iv, 28, 29.

[3] *Pol.*, iv, 516 a : " Hunc ergo gladium de manu Ecclesiæ accipit princeps, cum ipsa tamen gladium sanguinis omnino non habet. . . . Est ergo princeps sacerdotii quidam minister et qui sacrorum officiorum illam partem exercet quæ sacerdotii manibus videtur indigna."

fundamental difference between the legitimate prince
and the tyrant, which John now puts forward. The
supreme mark of distinction between the two is, he says,
the fact that the prince obeys the law and rules the people
by it, whereas the tyrant is never satisfied unless he nullifies the law's effect and reduces the people to slavery.[1]
Here John echoes St Isidore of Seville and writers of the
ninth century, but he gives the familiar distinction a fuller
meaning and draws from it a more far-reaching practical
conclusion. In the first place, the standard to which the
prince's own positive law (if we may use Austin's phrase)
must conform is the law of God. That law the prince
must have " before his eyes and in his heart," for it is both
written and unwritten: written, as in the Mosaic law,
unwritten, as imprinted on the clearer understanding of
the mind (*in puriore intelligentia mentis*).[2] So prevailing
is it that " the sanction of any law is vain unless it wear
the image of the divine law ; and no ordinance of a prince
is of any account unless it conform to the canons [*disciplinæ*]
of the Church." [3] Justinian himself borrowed from the
Mosaic law and bids the prince have recourse in his legislation to the tribe of Levi, which is the prototype of the
Christian priesthood. The prince should rely on the
clergy, the interpreters of divine law or equity (for John
goes near to the identification of the two), to help him make
his enactments consonant with that equity. In the second
place, the great strength and glory which the prince
possesses, the supreme power and authority that are his by

---

[1] iv, 513 c. *Cf.* viii, 777 d.

[2] iv, 522 d : " Prima quidem [lex] scribi potuit lapideis tabulis ; sed secunda
non imprimitur nisi in puriore intelligentia mentis."

[3] iv, 523 a : " Omnium legum inanis est censura, si non divinæ legis
imaginem gerat ; et inutilis est constitutio principis, si non est ecclesiasticæ
disciplinæ conformis. Quod et Christianissimum non latuit principem qui
legibus suis indixit ne dedignentur sacros canones imitari."

divine ordinance, making him an image of the divine majesty on earth, he holds for a definite purpose : he is endued with the authority of all that he may minister to the needs of all. Individuals have their own individual obligations, but upon him lie all the obligations of the community. To bear the universal burden he must have all the power which he thinks needful, so long as he will not use it contrary to justice.[1] His authority, therefore, while pre-eminent, he must not consider absolute ; and John quotes with approval Justinian's dictum that to submit the office of the Emperor to the sway of law is in fact greater than empire. Overshadowed therefore by the majesty of law natural, burdened with the obligation to procure the welfare of all his subjects, if he fails, the loss of his kingdom awaits him. " Sovereignty is transferred from people to people because of iniquities and deeds of violence, contumelies and different kinds of falsehoods." Both here and in the eighth book John is perfectly clear about the need of getting rid of tyrants—if they are not struck down by the hand of man they will be smitten by the hand of God—but he is not always very explicit about the particular crimes which merit the opposition of their subjects, and I am inclined to think that the interpretation put on the passages in question by later generations has led some writers to lay more emphasis upon his doctrine of tyrannicide than he himself would have done. The 'coherence' of head and members, the organic nature of the State, is, I think, the point of paramount importance in his eyes. In one passage he recognises that he has been some-

---

[1] iv, 513c : " In eoque præfertur ceteris [sc. princeps] quod, cum singuli teneantur ad singula, principi onera imminent universa. Unde merito in eum omnium subditorum potestas confertur, ut in utilitate singulorum et omnium exquirenda et facienda sibi ipse sufficiat et humanæ rei publicæ status optime disponatur, dum sunt alter alterius membra."

what severe on the prince and open to misinterpretation, for in the sixth book, under the more benign influence of Virgil, he inveighs against treason,[1] and even goes so far as to say that there are cases where the vices of the prince should be tolerated, if they do not actually amount to crimes ; [2] and he relates the amusing fable which Adrian IV told him, of the limbs which unsuccessfully revolted against the stomach, to show that it is better to bear with the harshness of a public authority which (to use his economic metaphor) distributes to all the consumers than to destroy the source of distribution and let the consumers starve.[3] These modifications, though they temper, scarcely, however, alter his main conclusion that the prince is emphatically not *legibus solutus*—absolved from the law; and in this, through the conception of a divine law or equity, he has arrived at a position which feudal lawyers reached by supposing the prince to be bound by the terms of a contract made to his people. To the feudal lawyer and to John alike the prince is bound by law, to the former because he is under contract with his vassals to protect their interests, to the latter because he is subject to that divine law of which all earthly law must be the interpretation.

But we must recur to the metaphor of the body. The heart, says John, is the senate, so called from its *senectus*, its age. But aged bodies are also infirm, so he hastens to add that he has in view the age of the mind rather than of the body ; for the age or maturity of the mind is, as he

---

[1] vi, 626 *d* : " Ceterum quod adversus caput aut universitatem membrorum dolo malo malitia præsumpserit, crimen est gravissimum et proximum sacrilegio, quia, sicut illud Deum attemptat, ita et istud principem, quem constat esse in terris quandam imaginem deitatis."

[2] vi, 629 *a*.

[3] vi, 625 *d* : " Longeque tutius esse ut ei quod distribuat ministretur quam illo [*sc.* stomacho] evacuato omnia membra esuriant. . . . Tale est, inquit, frater si recte attendas, in corpore rei publicæ ubi, licet plurimum appetat magistratus, non tam sibi quam aliis coacervat."

expresses it in a pregnant phrase, that wisdom which allots to each duty and obligation its proper place and makes the whole life a work of art.[1] Senators or councillors should be kept free from venality, and for this purpose the prince should see that they are not indigent. The same should apply to other public officials, whom he terms *quæstores* and *commentarienses*, that is, financial or exchequer officials of some kind and stewards of estates respectively, whom he compares to the belly and internal organs of the body ; [2] " for," he remarks, " it is impossible for a man to follow justice and money "—a pertinent comment on mediæval judicial methods and aims. It is hard to see whether for his senate John has in mind a standing professional council (he instances the Areopagus and the Roman Senate) or a council of great nobles present in virtue of their tenure and dignity. Probably the latter, for in the next paragraph he refers to councillors who are perpetually in attendance on the prince, the permanent secretariat, as we might say, and compares them to the *latera*, the sides. It is here most of all that corruption is to be avoided, for it is generally rife.[3] In an amusing section on the unscrupulousness of courtiers, which he professes to have experienced, John compares them to lawyers always wanting a refresher,[4] or to the doctors in the description of the medical school at Salerno, who treat you according to your ability to pay.[5]

[1] v, 560 d : " Ætas namque mentis sapientia est in qua omnium officiorum consistit distributio et artificium totius vitæ." " Denn die Weisheit ist eine Kunstübung des ganzen Lebens " (Gennrich).
[2] v, 540 c : " Quæstores et commentarienses (non illos dico qui carceribus præsunt, sed comites rerum privatarum) ad ventris et intestinorum refert imaginem." [3] v, 563 a.
[4] v, 564 b : " Qui nisi mulceantur obsequiis et reficiantur muneribus sibi fieri iniuriam suspicantur."
[5] v, 565 d. He quotes the words in some editions of the *Regimen Sanitatis* :

" Pro solis verbis montanis utimur herbis ;
Pro caris rebus pigmentis et speciebus."

71

Lawyers

The eyes, ears, and tongue are the governors of provinces. Their duties are primarily judicial.[1] This leads to an examination of the qualifications and duties of judges in a section which throws some light on John's legal training. The qualifications of a judge should be knowledge of law, strength of mind, and incorruptibility. He must be bound by oath to administer the law faithfully and rightly, unaffected by the claims of friendship or the need for haste. He must keep his temper and hide his emotions with an impassive face.[2] The discussion of procedure which follows shows the very strong influence of the Digest upon the author, whom Savigny praised for his remarkable knowledge of Justinian, the more remarkable because he was not a professional civilian.[3] Borrowed from the Digest is John's advice to the governor not to be familiar or to ' fraternise ' with the provincials, and above all not to let his passions and his personality obtrude.[4] The same advice should apply to " proconsuls, whom our people," he remarks, " usually call itinerant justices," though the name *justice* is wrong; " for, following after their own lusts in the pursuit of avarice and the robbery of poor folk, they wander from the path of equity." The justice should receive no money from the counties or from suitors for doing what is only his duty, and he must ask for hospitality only on a very small scale.[5]

[1] v, 567 c : " Præses igitur est qui in iure reddendo provincialibus præsidet."
[2] v, 576 a.
[3] *Geschichte des römischen Rechts im Mittelalter*, iv, 368. He may have listened to Robertus Pullus at Oxford. It is possible also that he knew the *Liber Pauperum* of Vacarius, who taught at Oxford. Cf. A. J. Carlyle, *Mediæval Political Theory in the West*, ii, 2–3, and Webb's prolegomena to *Pol.*, vol. i, p. xlv. His discussion of the relation of the prince's law to equity recalls the *Exceptiones Petri* and the Provençal rather than the Bolognese school of law.
[4] From *Dig.*, i, 18, 19.
[5] v, 577 a. The famous and much-disputed passage probably does not refer to the yearly journeys authorised in the statute of 1166, but to more occasional eyres such as we know to have taken place before that date.

72

He and other officials would do well to remember what the *Lex Julia de repetundis* enacted about corruption ; yes, and so would bishops, archdeacons, rural deans, and other ecclesiastical officials as well ; " of whom," he quaintly says, " some indeed labour in God's harvest well enough," but others " behave as if they were Thesiphone [*sic*] or Megæra sent up from the lower world to incite Thebes to crime." " Ask the king himself what he thinks about them and he will tell you that there is no evil in the Church which they do not perpetrate." [1] Henry II doubtless would—without being asked.

The hand of the State is either armed or unarmed. Armed, it is its military force ; unarmed, it is the officials and administrators in subordinate posts, chief among whom are the publicans or tax-collectors, who are like the young of locusts that eat up the green leaves. [2] In the armed hand or military force the chief place is given to the knight. Knights must be carefully chosen and carefully trained. They must not be *milites gloriosi*, who wear silk and return scarless home from a declined battle " to paint Troy over their wine cups," [3] but disciplined, hardy men who can fight the Welsh better than our Palatine earls. [4] And they must be serious-minded people. Pope Eugenius III said that the English would be preferable to all other peoples in whatever they put their hands to, if only they would take things seriously and frivol less ; [5] and the chapters which John devotes to the praise of discipline make it quite clear that it was this quality which he thought his

---

[1] v, 580 *b* and *d*.

[2] vi, 580 *c*.

[3] vi, 594 *d*. He adapts Ovid in the line " Et pingunt fluido Pergama tota mero."

[4] vi, 611 *d*.

[5] vi, 616 *c* : " Beatus Eugenius eam [*sc.* gentem] ad quæcunque vellet applicari dixit esse idoneam et præferendam aliis, *nisi levitas impediret*." Eugenius was scarcely *vir miræ simplicitatis* as he was described !

73

countrymen lacked. These knights should be bound by oath to serve the king, but their oath should oblige them no less to protect the Church. They should remember that by reverencing and serving God and God's order they promote the good of the prince. To God first, then to man, their loyalty is owing.[1]

Lastly come the feet. These are the husbandmen, the agricultural classes and the artisans, the providers of food and clothing and the necessaries of life. John makes no attempt to define their economic functions, but remarks that they are an integral part of the whole and that their interests should be protected. An afflicted and discontented populace is, as he wittily says, a sure sign that the prince has the gout.[2] But if it has no grievances to complain of, if the higher limbs can rely on the lower and the lower respond equally to the higher and all are " members one of another," then the safety and happiness of the State is assured.[3]

Having exhausted his metaphor, John looks about him to find some new illustration (for he has a pictorial mind) of the character and harmonised activities of the organic State. He finds it in nature, in the life of the bees. Ending his political chapters on a note of poetry, he quotes in full the famous passage from the fourth Georgic which depicts the work of the hive, its ideal division of labour, its common effort and spirit of self-sacrifice :

[1] vi, 601 b : " Hæc autem omni militiæ formula præscribenda est et implenda ut Deo primum fides debita, deinde principi et rei publicæ servetur incolumis."

[2] vi, 619 c : " Afflictus namque populus quasi principis podagram arguit et convincit."

[3] Ibid. : " Tunc autem totius rei publicæ salus incolumis præclaraque erit, si superiora membra se impendant inferioribus et inferiora superioribus pari iure respondeant, ut singula sint quasi aliorum ad invicem membra et in eo sibi quisque maxime credat esse consultum in quo aliis utilius noverit esse prospectum."

JOHN OF SALISBURY

Omnibus una quies operum, labor omnibus unus.

. . . . .

Sæpe etiam duris errando in cotibus alas
Attrivere, ultroque animam sub fasce dederunt ;
Tantus amor florum et generandi gloria mellis.
Ergo ipsas quamvis angusti terminus ævi
Excipiat (neque enim plus septima ducitur estas),
At genus immortale manet, multosque per annos
Stat fortuna domus et avi numerantur avorum.

The fervent, purposeful diligence of its citizens fascinates
him ; his comment on the line

Fervet opus, redolentque thymo fragrantia mella

is characteristic: " Thus its citizens are engaged in their
various callings, and while individuals pursue their own
work with the good of the whole community in view,
while justice is honoured and practised, the sweetness of
honey everywhere pervades its territories." [1]   He delights
in the analogy.   " Search all the writers who have ever
written on the State, read the histories of states themselves,
and you will never find civic life [*vita civilis*] more rightly
or more elegantly described." [2]   The care and attention
shown by the bees to their ' kings ' is not lost upon him ;
it makes him add some tolerant paragraphs to modify
his earlier and more uncompromising remarks about the
secular power.   " I am satisfied," he says, " that I have
given the civil power loyal shoulders for its support ; nor
do I merely bear it, but bear it with pleasure, so long as it
be subject to God and follow His order.[3]   Otherwise, if
it struggle against the divine commands and wish me to side
with it in a fight against God [*theomachia*] I freely reply

---

[1] vi, 621 *c* : " Ita variis tenentur occupationibus cives et dum sic coluntur
officia singulorum ut universitati prospiciatur, dum iusticia colitur, fines
omnium mellea dulcedo perfundit."
[2] vi, 620 *d*.
[3] vi, 626 *b* : " Dum Deo subiecta est et illius ordinem sequatur." *Ordo*
probably stands for the Church.

that God must be preferred to any man." [1]   The subjection of all the limbs to the head must be conditional upon the head's respecting conscience and scruple.   The reservation is always there.   All power is from God, and must be reverenced as such, but only so long as it obeys the divine will, and maintains the organ by which that will is communicated to men.   At this point it might seem natural for John to conclude.   But he does not.   By a transition which has been compared [2] to Dante's progress from the Inferno through Purgatory to a higher and purer region, he rises again from depicting the outward forms of political organisation and their relation to one another to the study of the inner and spiritual life of the individual member of the community.   The stars which he comes forth to see are the beacon-lamps of philosophy, the queen of knowledge, whose highest task is to unite mankind in the bond of truth and love to God.   He comes once more to the problem of conduct, and devotes the last two books to the answers which the great schools of philosophy made to the old question, the meaning of the good.   His aim is strictly practical ; for, as he says, *nichil virtute civilius* or, as we might paraphrase, goodness is more than anything else the bond of men in communities.   To its attainment every activity must be subordinated.   It is the aim of all reading, it is the aim of all research, and even when accurate and sure knowledge cannot be had and there are only probabilities to rely on, that probability should be accepted for true which leads to moral betterment. [3]   Thoroughly eclectic, he is ready to borrow from every school of thought, to choose out and adapt to his purpose, as Cicero did, tenets from them all.   They are all his clients, as he remarks at

---

[1] vi, 626 b.

[2] Schaarschmidt, *Johannes Saresberiensis*, p. 173.

[3] i, 388 b.   *Cf.* C. Prantl, *Geschichte der Logik im Abendlande*, ii (ed. 1885), 235.

the opening of his work ; he makes Academics, Stoics, and
Epicureans alike his slaves.[1]   The formal philosophers will
object, will protest against his violence, but he cannot
help being an anthologist.   Whatsoever things were
written, were written for his learning, and he refuses to
be kept within the compartments of one school.   I believe
that this helps to account for his dismissal of the Aristotelian
logic in one place as *astutiæ* ; perhaps for his disappointment when on revisiting St Geneviève after some years
he found his former colleagues there still " where they were
before," not advanced from their old position, still inspired
by the old aims ; [2] and for his refusal to accept the judgment of any one branch of philosophers on that large list
of " problems which a wise man may doubt " in the seventh
book of the *Metalogicus*.   It makes him incoherent at
times, tantalising, if you will, but his allusions, his borrow-
ings, his dips into history, keep you perpetually on the
alert.   Perhaps even the preoccupied Becket, campaigning
before Toulouse, may have found time now and then in
the evenings to read and ponder deeply John's praise of
the Epicurean ideal—the life of happy and undisturbed
tranquillity—that was not the life of camps and sieges and
ridings through Languedoc.   One passage may have
struck the Chancellor particularly.   John is praising the
simplicity of that ideal, and, addressing Becket, he says :
" I shall not forbid you to dress in raiment of gold, to dine
daily in splendid state, to be honoured above all ; if I may
put it tersely, to do as is customary to do in these degenerate
days, while remaining upright yourself, and to mock a
world that mocks you with its allurements.   For you are

[1] i, 387 *d* : " Omnes ergo qui michi in verbo aut opere philosophantes
occurrunt, meos clientes esse arbitror, et quod maius est, michi vendico in
servitutem."
[2] *Metalogicus*, ii, 805.

too great a man to be caught in its tentacles, though it has caught many thus. On your initiative, they say, under your guidance and leadership, the famous king of the English, Henry II, greatest of the kings of Britain if the results of his actions match their beginnings, is thundering in the neighbourhood of the Garonne ; and, successfully investing Toulouse, is not only frightening back the Provençals to the Rhone, but has also shaken with fear the princes of Spain and the Gauls by destroying strongholds and subduing peoples, threatening one and all. Amid such scenes of strife keep innocency, I beseech you, and behold and speak and proclaim equity. Decline not through love and hate, fear and hope, from the right path."[1] Did this, did the political teaching of the book penetrate the future martyr's mind more deeply than John ever hoped?[2] The Becket of ten years thence might have told : but he may have left us the answer written in his blood.

The doctrine that the prince is the servant of the priesthood, the difference between the legitimate ruler and the tyrant, the working out of the part to be played by each member of the organised body politic—these are the three principal contributions of the *Policraticus* to mediæval political theory. Each has its characteristic presentation, but only one perhaps can be called in any sense original and not an amplification of earlier theory. John of Salisbury arrives at his conclusion that the prince is the agent of the *sacerdotium* by an almost novel exposition of the familiar doctrine of the two swords. He declares that it was from the Church that the prince received the material sword, since to her both swords originally belonged. The material

---

[1] *Pol.*, viii, 821 *d*, 822 *a*.
[2] To speak of Becket as being " mit dem Geiste des *Policraticus* getränkt," as Gennrich (*op. cit.*, p. 158) does, is perhaps rather too great an assumption.

78

sword the prince wields for her use and profit, and consequently is her minister.[1]   Dr A. J. Carlyle, in a recent investigation of the passage, has pointed out parallels for this in St Bernard's *De Consideratione* and in one of his letters to Pope Eugenius III, and also in the *Summa Gloria* of the remarkable Honorius of Augsburg, written not long after the settlement of Worms.   But the passages in St Bernard, where he is urging Eugenius to draw the material sword against the obstinate and disorderly people of Rome or against the enemies of the Eastern Church, do not, Dr Carlyle considers, imply any intention on St Bernard's part to put forward a definite thesis of the relation of the temporal power to the spiritual.   Honorius, on the other hand, is more like John in definitely advancing a theory of their relations, though unlike John he relates the principle that both swords belong to the Church to the Donation of Constantine.   Now John's statement occurs in a general discussion of the difference between the prince and the tyrant, and the particular context is an examination of the relation of the prince to the law of God and the Church, to illustrate which he cites the humility of Constantine at the Council of Nice—Constantine declared that it was not lawful for a man who was subject to the judgment of the priests to examine the causes of those who were to be judged by God alone—and the excommunication and suspension of Theodosius from the regalia and insignia of empire by St Ambrose.   The safest conclusion would be that both in John of Salisbury and in Honorius of Augsburg we find the first definite statement that all authority, ecclesiastical or secular, belongs to the spiritual power.

Yet for all his sacerdotalism John is no bigot.   He is perfectly conscious of the defects in his own order and

[1] *Pol.*, iv, 331–334.

criticises them with uncommon shrewdness. This is clearly brought out in his account of a conversation he had with Adrian IV, who asked him what people really thought about the Pope and the Roman Church. His reply no Pope without a great sense of humour would have taken without offence. People were saying, he answered, that the Roman Church behaved like a stepmother rather than like a mother: that in it was a fatal vein of avarice, scribes and pharisees laying grievous burdens on men's shoulders, accumulating " precious furniture " (*pretiosam suppellectilem*), covetous to a degree: that the Holy Father himself was " burdensome and scarcely to be borne." The Pope —an Englishman—laughed; and, in a passage which Browning might have put into verse, told a parable of the stomach, and explained that the riches which the head of the Church accumulated went to supply the needs of the whole body. If John heard any more unpleasant things about the Pontiff he was to let him know at once.[1] John learned his lesson from the Pope's advice—*omnium utilitatem attende*: " cultivate a sense of proportion whether you criticise the Church or the secular power." For he is balanced in judgment, wide in his outlook, and that is what makes his work of permanent interest to his readers to-day. After the storms of the investiture struggle we seem to have reached sanity and quiet in a mind that is both academic and practical.

What then of the influence of the work? It would perhaps be possible to trace its effect on Nicolas of Cusa, when he develops his theory of the medicines which the body politic needed when diseased, and applies John's anthropomorphism to the Empire; or upon St

[1] *Pol.*, vi, 625 *b*: " Risit pontifex et tantæ gratulatus est libertati, præcipiens ut, quotiens sinistrum aliquid de ipso meis auribus insonaret, hoc ei sine mora nuntiarem."

Thomas when he asserts the priesthood to be the soul of the body politic. But these metaphors of the body were current ; theorists before and after John had them. Instead, I will merely take an instance of the practical application of John's definition of the State at a time of crisis a hundred years later. It is turned against Aymer, the bishop-elect of Winchester, and his Lusignan brothers in 1258 by the newly-arisen nationalist party led by de Montfort and Roger Bigod. In a letter which they and their fellow ' reformers,' on behalf of the community of England, addressed to the Pope after the flight of the foreigners, in order to justify their expulsion and to ask that Aymer should not return, they used the argument that the State was a body supported and governed in the way John had declared, and they stated it in the very terms which he used. They had proceeded against the Poitevins because the State should be an organic unity, and "in the one body it is not befitting that there should be lack of harmony in the members." [1] Here is the doctrine pressed into the service of an early nationalism, unless, of course, we take the statement to be the mere rhetoric of a pious and erudite scribe. But there was a strong doctrinaire element, however crude, in the baronial movement, and the definition of John of Salisbury suited it well.

M. Janet was probably right in seeing in John the inspirer of the political doctrine of the *Ligue* in France in the sixteenth century ; he terms it " that detestable theory which on the one hand pushes the hatred of the civil power as far as tyrannicide, and on the other hand exalts the despotism of priests." [2] It is perfectly true that John

---

[1] *Fœdera* (1816), i, 373 : "Nos igitur attendentes quod respublica corpus quoddam est ; quod divini muneris beneficio *etc.* . . . nec expedit quod in uno corpore dissonantia sit membrorum."
[2] *Histoire de la science politique*, i, 341.

had said that the tyrant was *plerumque occidendus*[1]—that he should generally be got rid of ; but in justification to John it must be said that this is not the essential part of his political theory, and that the *Ligueurs* did not give his doctrine of the commonwealth very careful consideration. Too much occupied in claiming their opponents as tyrants, they might perhaps have learned a lesson from the emphasis which he laid on the unity of the body politic or from the good-humoured advice which Adrian IV gave him : but here we touch the weakness of his and other sacerdotalist theories which emerges in their application by the opponents of Divine Right at the end of the Renaissance. Who is to decide when the prince ceases to be a legitimate prince and becomes a tyrant? Who, in fact, is to interpret the Divine Law, to call down the thunder and correction of immutable Equity on the offending head? It is the old, scarcely soluble question of sovereignty that arises, and men have ever answered it in different ways. But whatever is to be our own reply to that question, we can scarcely subscribe to the word " detestable." For the birth of modern political liberty is, as Dr Figgis has reminded us, to be found in the somewhat crude assertions made by dissenting religious bodies of their right to worship and hold their religious opinions unmolested by, and even sometimes to chastise, the Great Leviathan of the State. Those of us who are sufficiently old-fashioned and un-repentant to hold precious liberty of thought and dis-cussion in the sense in which John Stuart Mill understood it, those of us who are sufficiently advanced in view to claim autonomy for university, church, or guild, should not forget, or be ungrateful to, John of Salisbury. His anthropomorphism has been derided ; but, after all, he

[1] *Pol.*, viii, 778 *a*.

82

gave the State a soul, he made it human. To him it was a person, fallible, but with infinite potentiality for goodness : no machine, but a creature that breathed, thought, willed, dependent on all the delicate adjustments of the human body, the harmony and the rhythm that give strength and beauty. He applied to it the mediæval conception of personality, " the individual subsistence of a rational nature " ; he made it live indeed. The modern nation-state he could neither see nor foreshadow, yet his common-wealth—and in spite of his Roman terms he is perpetually thinking of England—has no small message for our com-munity to-day. " Tunc autem totius rei publicæ salus incolumis præclaraque erit, si superiora membra se im-pendant inferioribus et inferiora superioribus pari iure respondeant, ut singula sint quasi aliorum ad invicem membra."

E. F. JACOB

BIBLIOGRAPHY

A. PRIMARY SOURCES

Johannis Saresberiensis Opera omnia. Ed. J. A. Giles. 5 vols. Oxford, 1848. (Punctuation often inaccurate ; reproduced with still further errors in Migne, *Patrologia Latina*, cxcix.)

Johannis Saresberiensis Policraticus. Text with prolegomena, notes, and indices. Ed. C. C. J. Webb. 2 vols. Oxford, 1909. (The best edition.)

Further correspondence of John of Salisbury in *Materials for the History of Thomas Becket*, ed. J. C. Robertson, Rolls Series, v–vii, and in *Petrus Cellensis : Epistolæ*, in Migne, *Pat. Lat.*, ccii.

B. SECONDARY SOURCES

(a) Special Studies

H. F. REUTER : *Johann von Salisbury.* Berlin, 1842.

C. SCHAARSCHMIDT : *Johannes Saresberiensis nach Leben und Studien, Schriften und Philosophie.* Leipzig, 1862.

83

SOME GREAT MEDIÆVAL THINKERS

M. Demimuid : *Jean de Salisbury.* Paris, 1873.

P. Gennrich : *Staats- und Kirchenlehre Johanns von Salisbury.* Gotha, 1894.

(The studies of Schaarschmidt and Gennrich are the best.)

(b) John's Education and Literary Environment

H. F. Reuter : *Geschichte der religiösen Aufklärung des Mittelalters.* 2 vols. Berlin, 1875.

R. L. Poole : *Illustrations of the History of Mediæval Thought and Learning.* 1st ed., London, 1884 ; 2nd ed., London, 1920.

R. L. Poole : " The Masters of the Schools at Paris and Chartres in John of Salisbury's Time," *Eng. Hist. Rev.*, xxiv, p. 321.

G. Robert : *Les écoles et l'enseignement de la théologie pendant la première moitié du XIIème siècle.* Paris, 1909.

(Bishop) W. Stubbs : *Seventeen Lectures on the Study of Mediæval and Modern History.* London, 1886. Lectures VI, VII.

H. Rashdall : *The Universities of Europe in the Middle Ages,* vol. i. Oxford, 1895.

(c) His Philosophy

B. Hauréau : *Histoire de la philosophie scolastique.* Paris, 1872–80.

C. von Prantl : *Geschichte der Logik im Abendlande,* vol. ii (2nd ed.). Leipzig, 1885.

M. de Wulf : *Histoire de la philosophie médiévale.* Louvain, 1905.

Otto von Gierke : *Political Theories of the Middle Age.* Tr. and ed. Maitland. Cambridge, 1900.

R. W. and A. J. Carlyle : *Mediæval Political Theory in the West,* vols. iii (London, 1915) and iv (London, 1922).

P. Janet : *Histoire de la science politique,* vol. i. Paris, 1872.

On the comparison of the State to a body *cf.* :

F. W. Maitland : *Collected Papers,* vol. iii. Cambridge, 1911. Papers on " The Crown as Corporation " and " The Body Politic."

Light may be thrown on John's knowledge of Roman law by :

C. Wendt : *Magister Vacarius.*

H. Fitting : *Juristische Schriften des früheren Mittelalters.*

P. Vinogradoff : *Roman Law in Mediæval Europe.*

IV

ST THOMAS AQUINAS AND THE PAPAL
MONARCHY

THE thirteenth century, in which St Thomas Aquinas lived, was a time when the Papal Monarchy, as a political institution, was a fact of the first order in the social organisation of Europe. It was an institution known to St Thomas both as a territorial sovereignty related to other secular kingdoms and as the seat of a universal spiritual jurisdiction claiming and wielding a supreme authority above them all. We have to consider in this paper the theory of monarchy as traced by St Thomas, and, in particular, the position of the Roman Pontiff among the other rulers of the world.

But, in order to appreciate his views more readily, it will be useful for us to have some slight sketch of the man himself, and of the general outlook of the period in which he lived. These may help us to follow the turn of his thought, and to understand the intensity of conviction with which he could hold to a point of view so entirely foreign to that of our own time.

The thirteenth century was a period of large and varied achievement. It was a time in which high ideals—religious, political, civic, academic—flourished : a time of chivalry, knightly and spiritual alike. It witnessed the early days and development of the orders of St Francis and St Dominic. It saw the burghers of the towns, merchants and traders, growing more conscious of inherent power ;

municipalities grouping themselves together for their mutual advantage. Events, forerunners of the seams and cracks that would ultimately break it up, were already taking place within the great fabric of feudalism which dominated the whole of Europe, binding it into a unity in which every man had his appointed place, like a cog or a wheel in an immense machine. The time was a focus for a wonderful display of artistic brilliance, when cathedrals like those of Chartres, Paris, Salisbury, and Lincoln were in the building or brought to completion. It was a period of schools and universities—a golden age of Paris and Oxford, Bologna, Cologne, Salerno, Naples—where immense throngs of students drank in a culture fast evolving to the highest point of its development. Socially and politically institutions were developing and becoming consolidated, fluid theories were coming to crystallisation, and the seal of a new synthesis of thought, the outcome of a higher civilisation and a broader outlook upon life, was being stamped upon every department of human speculation and endeavour.

This was taking place in the midst of all the movement, the social and political disturbances, of an unrestful and turbulent age. There were the comings and goings of armies and the clash of battles. There was a continual ferment and seething of opinions in the schools. There were the rank abuses and the reforms within the Church itself. Throughout all this there was shaping an edifice of thought in which the whole created universe was to be embraced, with all that the created universe means and implies. This was at once to be a theology, a science, and a philosophy ; and the stones of which it was built were quarried in the open mine of revelation and from the very depths of the understanding of the human spirit itself. Such was the concept and the ideal of what is the most lasting monument of the thirteenth century—the finished product of scholasticism.

It would be out of place here to elaborate in any detail the relations and reactions of philosophy and theology during this period of criticism and synthesis ; but it must be pointed out that, while closely interwoven in their works, the philosophy of the schoolmen is capable of standing alone without the support of theology. We shall see how St Thomas, borrowing principles from the latter, treats his political theory in a thoroughly philosophical way.

Considered, then, as a philosophy, scholasticism extended to moral, social, political, and economic problems and their solutions as well as to logical, metaphysical, and psychological ones. It was not an isolated movement, divorced from other movements of the age ; but one—perhaps the most complete, as it was the most significant—manifestation of the general spiritual culture of mediævalism. It marked the culmination of an epoch in civilisation.

One point in the movement of cultural development, gathering force in the preceding centuries, almost irresistible in the thirteenth, is noteworthy. It is striking in the evidences we have of the spirit of the times : apparent alike in the conception of the cathedrals, in the literature of the period, in the aspirations and constitutions of the communal brotherhoods of the friars, in the philosophy of the schoolmen. In all these there is to be found a great diversity of detail transfused by a singleness of purpose and a unity of plan. No two of the great mediæval churches, for example, are alike. Each is characteristically itself— unlike any other, as one human personality differs from all others. Yet these mediæval churches evidence a fundamental identity, a singleness of conception and of aim, which makes them one despite the manifold divergencies in which it is realised. Their artistic unity was the expression of the spirit of man orientated toward God, with whom it literally felt itself to be in closest contact. So was it also for the exalted hymns and proses, the sermons and prayers, which are characteristic of the time ; so for the fresh manifestation of the religious life in the mendicant orders. And a similar structural and fundamental unity is to be discovered in the works of the schoolmen. The philosophy of any given period is at once the outcome and the expression, as it is the interpretation, of its civilisation, and, above all, of the causes which brought that civilisation into being. The scholasticism of the thirteenth century is a master-key to the understanding of mediævalism. Some of its metaphysical principles, in particular, provide an explanation of the Thomistic conception of the Papal Monarchy.

Like all the other expressions of the movement of the spirit which was then taking place, this philosophy found its basis clearly and distinctly in God and in the principle of final causes. Everything in nature is orientated by its very essence toward the source of its being. This principle, it should be emphasised, was a philosophical, and not a theological one. But like the theological and mystical manifestations of the same orientation in religious orders and cathedral builders, in craftsmen and poets, in missionaries and crusaders, it is a principle of prime importance for our understanding of the political theory of St Thomas with regard to the Pope, and the general acceptance in practice of his monarchy, no matter how mystical or how remote it may appear to be to-day. The passion for a complete unification in knowledge, at all times a characteristic of the human mind, is nowhere to be seen more thoroughly or more effectually displayed than in scholasticism ; and there not least notably in the works of St Thomas Aquinas.

The foregoing presents a necessarily condensed and therefore extremely eclectic summary of an outlook on the thirteenth century. We have now to draw a very rapid sketch of St Thomas himself.

Aquinas was born at Rocca Sicca, on the confines of the kingdoms of Sicily and Campania, in 1227. His house had been of strong Imperial traditions which were continued in the persons of his brothers, who both became knights in the service of the Emperor. Blood relative of kings and of emperors, Thomas was cradled in luxury ; and he received his earliest education in the great Benedictine house of Monte Cassino, to which he was sent when he was five years old. Here he remained, during the impressionable years of childhood, until he was twelve. But more influences than monastic ones played their part in this formative period of his life. The age was a rough one ; and the sanctuary of Monte Cassino was not spared from its violence. Aquinas knew of the ravages of war by hearsay, for the Abbey was deeply involved in the quarrels between the Pope and the Emperor. But he had to learn of them by personal experience as well. While Abbot Stephen, shrewd enough to believe that the Pope was for the moment on the losing side, was away in Lombardy currying favour with the excommunicated Emperor, a band of the Imperial soldiers stormed and captured the Abbey, the monks of which they drove out or murdered. And Aquinas took refuge with his family. The sack of Monte Cassino was the occasion of his going to Naples, where he astonished his new teachers by the profoundness of his understanding, the keenness of his logical faculty, and the prodigious grasp of his memory. It is said of him that he never forgot or failed to understand what he had once read. He had everything in life—honours, rank, position either in Church or in State—to look forward to ; yet, while still a mere lad and a student at Naples, he elected to join the lately established begging fraternity of St Dominic. This proposal aroused such violent opposition on the part of his relatives that, when prayers and entreaties proved of no avail, resort was had to sterner means to dissuade him from his purpose. He was kidnapped and imprisoned in the family fortress. And this opposition only came to an end when both the Emperor and the Pope intervened, and he was allowed to carry out his wishes.

The history of St Thomas, from the time he left his home in the habit of a friar, is one of amazing academic success. To his native mental gifts of penetration and retention he added an extraordinary resolution and an intense application to study. His religious superiors were not slow to appreciate these qualities and turn them to the best advantage. He was sent to Cologne to become a student under Albert the Great ; and, when Albert left Cologne for Paris, Thomas accompanied him, as he did again on the return of the master to his former university. But in 1252 he was sent to Paris as sub-regent in the Dominican school there ; and shortly afterward received his licence to teach. At this period considerable opposition was shown to the friars on the part of the secular teachers of the university. The causes of friction were doubtless considerable. They came to a head on the occasion of a brawl between students and the city guard, in which one of the former was killed. Satisfaction for the outrage was refused by the city. Thereupon, as a protest, the university suspended its lectures. But the friars kept their schools open ; and refused to agree to a proposal of the secular masters that no one should be admitted to the doctorate who would not bind himself by oath to suspend his lectures in the event of any similar circumstances arising. St Thomas, in consequence, was not admitted to his doctorate in theology until 1257.

Other and more serious attacks were made upon the friars ; and ultimately the whole question had to be referred to the Pope at Anagni, whither Aquinas betook himself to plead the cause of the religious in person.

But it was rather by his astounding success in the academic sphere that he arrested the attention not only of the Pope but of the entire learned world. He returned to the University of Paris ; but we find him also at Rome, Bologna, Orvieto, and Perugia, called by the Pope to teach at the papal court. He was even once in England, where he attended a chapter of his Order in London. He left Paris finally for Naples to organise the *studium generale* there ; and he died on his way to Lyons, whither he had been summoned by Gregory X to take part in the deliberations of the council to be held in that city. He was only forty-seven.

Such, in briefest compass, is a sketch of the career of St Thomas. It reveals him to us as related to kings and emperors, the intimate of Popes, a great traveller, a keen observer of current affairs, and an outstanding figure in the schools. It shows him as one who was well acquainted with the actual political conditions of the Europe of his time.

We have now to consider, in part, what those conditions were, and to outline the theory maintained by St Thomas as to what they ought to be. The Papal Monarchy, as it existed in the thirteenth century, was a matter of fact and of historical necessity. It will not be necessary in this paper to deal at length with the well-known causal factors which operated in elevating the throne of the Fisherman to the highest apex amidst those of earthly sovereigns:— the events which suggested the legendary Donation of Constantine, the removal of the seat of Empire to the East, the Gift of Pepin, the long strife over the question of investitures, the triumph of Hildebrand, the emancipation of the Church from the royal power, and the definite defeat of Frederick in the thirteenth century. These are landmarks in the history of the Papacy. The Popes might conceivably have remained fishermen with St Peter and still fulfilled the high duties of their office, governing, in the name of Him whose place they filled on earth, a kingdom not of this world, and guiding its citizens, despite the world, to the triumph of their citizenship in eternity. But in that case, humanly speaking, the Church could never have been catholic. And such was not the fact. Neither was it the ideal of St Thomas, who saw through all the excesses and disorders of contemporary society a harmony and unity which should dominate it, which were inherently necessitated by the very ends for which any perfect society is formed.

While such causal factors as those to which allusion has been made operated, there were contemporary reasons why men should see in the Papacy the highest seat of spiritual power and accept the Papal Monarchy as a quite commonplace matter of fact. Long before, indeed, it had come to be that.

Subsidiary causes had also played their part. Of these the intercommunication throughout the world between the Pope and his bishops, necessary for the well-being of the Church and almost impossible except to it, was one.

Another was the rise of learning, which placed immense power in the hands of the clergy. The Cluniac reform was a third. There were many of these historic necessities making for the same end. And in the time of St Thomas a culture had come about in which a general acceptance of Rome as the supreme arbiter of affairs was a natural enough part. The practical assertion of the meaning and value of individual human life in the person of the citizen, the laws providing for the freeing of the serf, and the essential democracy of the friars contributed to this. The rising into power of municipalities and university corporations; the recognition of the duties of overlords toward vassals and the dependence of these upon the loyalty of the latter; the beginning of self-reliance and self-sufficiency among the merchant classes; the position of the craftsmen in the guilds and the pride of the artisan in his own craftsmanship; these were all causes of a realisation of personal worth and independence which could only have as effect the turning of men's minds toward their own inherent dignity. The canon law which protected them was the common law of the land throughout Christian Europe. In the thoroughly Catholic atmosphere in which they lived and thought the sum total of the impinging forces could only result in their orientation toward the centre of Christian unity. For that inherent human dignity and worth, consistently preached and taught by the Church, had its meaning only in the spiritual character of man and his ultimate spiritual destiny. The high claims made on behalf of the Papacy drew their strength from the developing cultural civilisation of individuals, with all the moral, social, and religious aspirations which such civilisation implied. This was justified by the metaphysical doctrine of the schoolmen, who recognised in the individual the only thing of any worth, the only true value, indeed the only thing that could be said to exist at all.

Another cause similarly influencing the mediæval conception of the Papacy can be traced to the universal passion for unity, already noticed as apparent in the expression of the spirit of the age alike in scholasticism, in artistic activity, and in the religious life of the friars. This unity was working itself out amid the greatest diversity in the various phases of social and political life. It drew its inspiration, in no small measure, from the common unity of belief in Christianity. In turn, the theoretical exposition of the social and political order found its basis in the unique conception of the God of Christian revelation as the end of all created things. This conception is fundamental. The characteristic note of scholastic ethics in the widest sense, in which the social, political, and economic are included, is emphatically that of finality. Consequently, all the manifold social and political relationships into which the individual can enter must be regulated by this far-reaching principle. We have seen that scholasticism insisted upon a strictly individualistic view of the universe. The individual alone exists and is of value. He alone can merit or can sin. Consequently upon this view, the social and political order into which he enters as an integral part must exist not for itself only, but for the sake of the individuals who compose it. This is at once the metaphysical and the ethical basis of, as it is the psychological outlook upon, the whole Thomistic social and political theory. Man—the individual—who is by nature a social animal, must find the end of his nature furthered by the society of which he necessarily forms a part. The furthering of this natural end, the completing and perfecting of his personality, is the work of the State, or indeed of any

94

social group into which he enters. The State thereby becomes a means toward the realisation of the full natural self-expression of the individual, by making possible a mutual co-operation of activities for the common good. In like manner, it may be remarked in parenthesis, that other perfect society, the Church, is the means for the realisation of the supernatural end of man.

These philosophical principles had found practical realisation in the older religious communities from the very beginning. They had come to practical expression in the co-operation of burghers in the towns, of masters and scholars in the universities, of craftsmen of the mediæval fine arts in the guilds. They became theoretically articulate and of universal application in the moral, social, and political doctrine of the school.

Aquinas is quite definite in his teaching upon the point. He is clear as to his definition of a person as the individual substance of a rational nature. He is explicit as to the end or purpose of society, or the State, which is the same as that of each person who enters into it ; [1] and this is the greater good of each in the virtuous life. He is no less explicit in regard to the source of the authority to govern,[2] which is a necessity for the common good once society is organised. This source of authority is God, the supreme Governor of all things.[3] From God the legitimate authority to govern passes to the whole group of individuals concerned ; and they, in turn, may constitute one, or several, of themselves as their representative in this matter.[4] The people, under God, are sovereign. They may, according to circumstances, entrust their sovereignty to a king or monarch, to an

---

[1] *De Regimine Principum*, lib. i, c. 14.
[2] *Summa Theol.*, Iª 2ᵃᵉ, Q. XCIII, a. 3.
[3] *De Regimine Principum*, lib. i, c. 1–3.
[4] *Summa Theol.*, Iª 2ᵃᵉ, Q. XC, a. 3.

95

aristocracy, or to a republican form of government. His own personal choice, based upon psychological reasons, is a compromise. He prefers a state or kingdom in which the power is given to one president, who has under him others also possessing powers of government. And he shows that a government such as this is in reality one shared by all the people, since all are eligible to govern, and since the rulers are chosen by them all.[1] This, he says, is the best form of polity : partly kingdom, in so far as there is one president ; partly aristocracy, in so far as many have authority ; and partly democracy or popular government, for the rulers can be elected from the people, and to the people belongs the choice of their rulers.[2] The conception is that of a limited monarchy, in which both the ruler and his subordinates are chosen by the people. The principle involved is one of solidarity and unity, in which all the individual citizens, from the supreme ruler downward, each according to his office, conspire together toward a single end, which is the greatest absolute natural good of each one of them. This it is the *duty* of the monarch to set himself to bring about, in the several ways to which St Thomas alludes in his *Government of Princes*, as, for example, the securing of internal and external peace and moral order, the provision of a sufficiency of common necessaries for the people, and the like. Peace is the great desideratum in order that man should develop and attain his natural end. This being a duty on the part of the ruler, it is clear, as St Thomas indicates, that the king exists for the sake of the kingdom (*i.e.*, its individual members) and not the kingdom for the sake or advantage of the king.[3]

---

[1] *Summa Theol.*, I^a 2^æ, Q. cv, a. I.

[2] Aquinas has a caveat as to the qualifications of political knowledge on the part of the electorate necessary for the rational use of their powers in elections.   [3] *De Regimine Principum*, lib. iii, c. II.

And this is true for every kind of human society—the religious community presided over by the superior, the diocese administered by the bishop, the kingdom ruled by the monarch, the Church at large governed by the Pope. Each exists for the good of its members. And the rights and correlative duties of each member are determined by the end for which it exists. St Thomas's political doctrine is thus seen to be a distinct advance upon that of Aristotle, from whose recently translated *Politics* he borrowed much of his theory. By Aristotle the State was regarded as prior to and more important than the individual, whose duty was to become a good citizen and thus further the end of the State to which he was subordinated. For St Thomas, on the contrary, the position is reversed. It is the duty of the individual citizen to become a good man ; and the State is regarded as an instrument to be employed to this end. In it the true value of human personality, as far as this is naturally attainable, can be realised.

To be sure, the official teaching of the Church had always insisted upon the obedience to be paid by the citizen to the civil power. The things of Cæsar were to be rendered to Cæsar. Thus the Church was always an upholder of State authority. St Thomas, of course, does not oppose this teaching in any way ; but he lays stress on an instrumental conception of the State just referred to, and makes it the pivot of his political doctrine.

St Thomas's picture is utopian. The states with which he was familiar were not so consistently perfect as that. Yet signs pointing in the direction of his theory were not wanting. Coronations of kings, elections of Emperors and Popes, contractual oaths of fealty, pacts like the Great Charter of England, and elective representation of individuals in friary, university, Church, and State, were tendencies toward his ideal. We shall see later how the Pope comes into a still higher unity in his theory. The unification of individual interests in social groups such as cities and the federation of these in kingdoms was a practical cause contributing to the popular view of the Papacy.

A further cause lay in the organisation of government and discipline within the Church itself. Quite apart from their belief in it as a truth of revelation, it was easy for men to accept a supreme spiritual power, who were accustomed to the exercise of spiritual jurisdiction deriving from a higher source. They were familiar with appeals to religious superiors upon a lower plane ; and they accepted the appeal to Rome as final in these matters. We can appreciate the immense political importance that was attached to the power of investiture, for example, by princes the lonely outposts of whose growing empires were bishoprics far-flung upon the borders of their marches, as we can that of keeping powerful dioceses and wealthy abbeys subservient to their will and compliant to their demands. But the bishops of these outposts and rich dioceses *were* bishops, and enmeshed in the net of ecclesiastical organisation. Used to subserve the Imperial policy, they were also— and primarily—members of that universal society whose head, the *servus servorum Dei*, was the recognised supreme spiritual authority in Western Christendom. Their spiritual allegiance was due to him. So was it again in the case of the friars in their allegiance to Rome. They were directly dependent on the Holy See. Their influence also was enormous ; and their activity in missionary work brought home to the common folk—and particularly to townspeople—the pre-eminence of the Apostolic Throne even as a sort of secular world-power. Men's vision passed from their local horizon to the Pope. The temper and mentality of the period were one, by reason of causes such as these, which inclined them to look to the Papacy as a domination *de jure* as well as *de facto* superior to that of all purely secular rulers whatever.[1]

All the influences were everywhere making for a unitary conception of society as a whole, in which each individual had his own niche, and in which the inherent rights of each were, at least theoretically, respected. The high spiritual ideal of Augustine, as set forth in *The City of God*, had not lost its power to inflame the imagination and enthral the minds of men. The age of Aquinas still resounded with the echoes of his sublime words. Dante had not yet penned his arguments for a universal secular world-empire. Yet the unifying principle of his " Monarchy " was already alive. St Thomas gives us the argument by which we are able to weave all the threads of the secular and religious development of mediævalism, to several of which allusion has been made in this paper, into the texture of his political theory.

It may be repeated that, for St Thomas as for scholastics generally, the universe is conceived to be focussed upon a point, and that point God. Without a realisation of that fundamental note of scholasticism all its harmony is meaningless, its coherence illusory, its system—and especially its moral, social, and political system—absurd. It would be just as impossible to understand the spiritual life and culture of the thirteenth century without realising what God meant to those who lived it, as to understand its philosophy without this, its central core.

The thought of Aquinas, carrying us beyond his theory as to the constitution of kingdoms, may fairly be presented

[1] The power of the Papacy was so tremendous that what Wells (in *The Outline of History*) calls " the Reformation according to the Princes " was simply a reaction against it.

as follows. He borrows three points from theology : that man has been raised to a supernatural order ; that Christ was God ; and that He established a spiritual social body to which Christians belong, viz., the Catholic Church, of which the Pope is the supreme ruler.

For St Thomas, then, the whole universe consists of an interrelated and organised hierarchy of individuals ; and all of these tend, each according to its nature, toward God, the Sovereign Creator and Lord of all. Included in this universe is man, who is made in the likeness of his Creator, the crown and end of the creation. But man is a composite being, formed of spirit as well as matter ; and, though he is bound now by the limits of space and of time, yet he has a destiny beyond the cramping limitations of either. The Christian man is ordained not only toward a natural end intrinsic to himself, which he might conceivably attain in the conditions of merely human society ; but, in virtue of his spiritual nature, he has a supernatural end as well. This extrinsic end consists in his union with God in the Beatific Vision. It can be attained only through a life of grace and at the price of the exercise of virtue, in which his salvation must be worked out in the society of his fellow men. Thus man belongs to two orders, that of nature and that of grace. As a member of the order of nature, he looks to the rule and authority of the temporal sovereign, whose function and duty it is to provide him with the means necessary to the consecution of his natural end in the social State. As a member of the supernatural commonwealth, he is provided for by the organisation and ministrations of the Christian Church, whose ruler, the Pope, represents Christ Himself upon earth.

" The natural end of a people formed into a society," St Thomas writes, " is to live virtuously ; for the end of any society is the same as that of the individuals composing it. But since the virtuous man is also determined to a further end, the purpose of society is not merely that man should live virtuously, but that by virtue he should come to the enjoyment of God." [1]   He goes on to argue that, if this end could be attained by means of the natural capacities of men alone, it would be the duty of the king to direct them toward it—"for a king is one to whom is committed sovereign power over human affairs."   But the end extrinsic to man's nature, the possession of God, is not to be obtained by the exercise of any purely natural capacities.   In consequence, it cannot belong to any merely human direction of those capacities to bring it about.   This belongs to the divine government ; and "this government pertains to that King who is not only man, but God, namely our Lord Jesus Christ. . . . The administration of this Kingdom has been committed, not to the kings of this world, but to priests, in order that the spiritual should be distinct from the temporal ; and above all to the Sovereign Roman Pontiff, the Successor of Peter, the Vicar of Christ, to whom all the kings of Christian people should be subject as to our Lord Jesus Christ Himself."

The reason of this is that whoever has the care of proximate or antecedent ends should be directed or governed by him whose business it is to lead men to their ultimate end, since all these intermediate ends are no more than means toward reaching the last one. " The good life, or life of justice, which men live on earth," he argues further, " tends to the blessed life, for which we hope in heaven, as to its end ; as in the same way the well-being of a society bends to its purpose all the particular good things which are acquired by men—for example, riches, health, eloquence,

[1] *De Regimine Principum*, lib. i, c. 14.

or erudition." Consequently, since the ruler whose
business it is to direct men to their ultimate end should
be placed over those who have the care only of intermediate
ends related to that final one, " it is evident that the king
should be subject to and obey that authority which is placed
in the hands of the priest."

He points out, as a consequence of this, that it is a *duty*
incumbent on the king to see that his subjects observe
their obligations in the life of virtue, and to procure this
observance by the authority of his government. This, of
course, involves the correlative rights of legislative and
executive power ; the theory of which, with its metaphysical, moral, and psychological implications, is developed
at length in the *Summa Theologica*.[1] And we need not
dwell upon it here.

But a point which is of great importance in this connexion
is the doctrine of St Thomas that the " authority which is
placed in the hands of the priest " is not merely a spiritual
but also a temporal one.[2] This follows from the principles
already laid down. For the relation of the good life of
nature to the supernatural life of blessedness as a means
to an end is one which necessitates the supervision of the
means by that ruler whose principal concern is with the
end. Consequently, St Thomas argues that the Supreme
Pontiff is to be obeyed before all other rulers whatsoever as
well in those matters which regard civil well-being as in
those which relate directly to the salvation of souls.[3] It
has just been said that the rights of rulers are grounded upon
duties ; and it belongs to the office of the Pope to see that

---

[1] *Summa Theol.*, Iᵃ 2ᵃᵉ, QQ. xc–c.
[2] " As the body has being, power, and action by reason of the soul . . .
so also the temporal jurisdiction of princes by reason of the spiritual jurisdiction of Peter and his successors " (*De Regimine Principum*, lib. iii, c. 10).
Though this passage was not written by St Thomas, it conveys his teaching.
[3] *In Quatuor Libros Sententiarum*, lib. ii, dist. xliv, *in fine*.

those duties are not so performed by secular monarchs as to frustrate the very purpose for which the rights were conferred. Hence it is within his supreme power to visit with punishment anyone whomsoever for his offences or crimes; and, it would follow, to absolve his subjects from their allegiance to an unjust or evil prince. The writer of the third book of *The Government of Princes* is careful to add a caveat, " in the full spirit of Thomas," [1] explicitly limiting papal jurisdiction to cases which involve a matter of sin.

Thus St Thomas solved the apparent dualism, intolerable to the mediæval philosophical mind, as it was foreign to the whole temper and cultural spirit of the time, between the two orders of sovereignty temporal and spiritual. There were two orders of kingship, and the spiritual was supreme. To it all kings of Christian peoples should be subject. There were two social orders, worldly and religious, as there were two ends for man to reach, the natural and the supernatural. But these orders were not mutually exclusive or incompatible; because, since the natural end of man is subordinated to the supernatural, it is completed and perfected—not destroyed—by the latter. Citizen of both Church and State, the Christian man may be said to be not really in two, but in one great social organisation, the parts, indeed, of which can be distinguished, but whose unity is achieved by reason of the last and supernatural end of man. This was the theory of St Thomas. It was a philosophical justification of the belief of his contemporaries, as it was also that of the actual political situation of the time.

There is one point upon which I have scarcely touched, except in passing, in this paper. And this, principally, because Aquinas himself does not seem to have treated it.

[1] Dunning, *A History of Political Theories, Ancient and Mediæval*, p. 206.

I refer to the territorial sovereignty of the Popes. Un-doubtedly, St Thomas was aware that the Pope was a territorial monarch. Legally, the Popes had been landed proprietors from the time of Constantine. Their estates had increased until they became rulers *de facto*, if not *de jure*. And, since Christian kings certainly came under their spiritual jurisdiction, it would be only a step forward in theory to invest them with kingship as of right. And this right they had actually possessed since the days of the Carlovingians. But the so-called ' Roman Question ' could hardly have interested Aquinas, in the form in which we are familiar with it, since it did not present itself in his time. Yet it would follow from his principles that the Sovereign Pontiff must be a temporal king as well as a priest. For the Pope, as supreme ruler of a society includ-ing kings and their subjects alike, must possess all those means which are necessary for the good government of his Church. Hence, as an inherent right of his office, he must be a territorial prince. We may take as a text in this connexion a passage from the third book of *The Government of Princes*. It is not certain by whom this book was written; but it fairly interprets what I conceive to be the view of Aquinas in the passages already cited or commented upon.

The author says that the temporal was joined to the spiritual Kingdom of Christ in the time of Blessed Sylvester; that the latter—the spiritual—is necessary for Christians, while the former is only a secondary necessity as minister-ing (*administrans*) to it.[1]

We may ask how the temporal kingdom of the Popes was conceived of as ministering to the spiritual Kingdom. And we may answer this with other questions. How was

---

[1] *De Regimine Principum*, lib. iii, c. 16.

the "Sovereign Roman Pontiff to whom all kings should be subject" going to live? Was he to be like St Peter, a fisherman—or a wanderer upon the earth? Was he to be a 'nobody's man' in the days of feudalism, when every man had his place in the definite structure of social organisation? Such a thing would have been as incredible as it was impossible in Catholic Europe. Could he then be a follower in the train of some great potentate, directing the affairs of Christendom as a dependent upon an overlord? There was no one in Europe great enough to be the patron of the Pope. He must at least, then, be a landed proprietor, himself great enough and powerful enough to secure the adequate administration of the vast affairs of the Church. And yet, as landed proprietor, he must be either subject or sovereign. But who could be the sovereign of the Pope? No one in the thirteenth century either was or claimed to be.

The historical necessities which brought the Papal Monarchy into being made of the Pope also a territorial sovereign; and, if the political view of St Thomas is rightly argued from the principles he lays down, he would have justified it as of theoretical necessity as well. With this reflection I may fittingly bring to a close this impression of the attitude of mind of the thirteenth century toward the Papacy and the theory of St Thomas concerning the Papal Monarchy. I say "impression" advisedly; since, in a paper of this kind, it is impossible to give a detailed and documented study of the subject. I have attempted to do no more than convey an impression of the man and the time which has been made on my own mind by studies, philosophical and theological rather than historical, which have extended over a number of years.

F. AVELING

BIBLIOGRAPHY

A. Primary Sources

S. Thomæ Aquinatis Opera. Summa Theologica ; Summa de Veritate Catholicæ Fidei contra Gentiles ; De Regimine Principum ; Commentaria in Libros Sententiarum. Parmæ, 1852.

Acta Sanctorum Martii a Joanne Bollando, S.J., etc. Parisiis et Romæ, MDCCCLXV.

Denifle-Chatelain : *Chartularium Universitatis Parisiensis.* Paris, 1889.

B. Secondary Sources

Baumann, J. J. : *Die Staatslehre des h. Thomas von Aquino.* 1873.

Cronin, M. : *The Science of Ethics.* Dublin, 1909.

De Wulf, M. : *Histoire de la philosophie médiévale.* 2nd ed. Louvain, 1905.

De Wulf, M. : *Philosophy and Civilisation in the Middle Ages.* London, 1922.

Dunning, W. A. : *A History of Political Theories, Ancient and Mediæval.* London, 1919.

Feugueray, H. R. : *Essais sur les doctrines politiques de Saint Thomas d'Aquin.* Paris, 1857.

Janet, P. A. R. : *Histoire de la science politique dans ses rapports avec la morale.* Paris, 1872.

Kennedy, D. J. : Article " Thomas Aquinas " in *Catholic Encyclopedia.* New York, 1913.

Mandonnet, P. F. : *Des écrits authentiques de S. Thomas d'Aquin.* Fribourg, 1910.

Molenaer, S. P. (ed.) : *Li livres du gouvernement des rois.* New York, 1899.

Penty, A. J. : *A Guildsman's Interpretation of History.* London, 1920.

Penty, A. J. : *The Restoration of the Guild System.* London, 1921.

Poole, R. L. : *Illustrations of the History of Mediæval Thought and Learning.* 2nd ed. London, 1920.

Rashdall, H. : *The Universities of Europe in the Middle Ages.* Oxford, 1895.

Rickaby, J. : *Aquinas Ethicus.* London, 1892.

Sertillanges, A. D. : *S. Thomas d'Aquin.* Paris, 1910.

Taylor, H. O. : *The Mediæval Mind.* London, 1911.

Touron, A. : *La vie de S. Thomas d'Aquin, avec un exposé de sa doctrine et de ses ouvrages.* Paris, 1740.

Vaughan, R. B. : *The Life and Labours of Saint Thomas of Aquin.* London, 1871.

Walsh, J. J. : *The Thirteenth, Greatest of Centuries.* New York, 1915.

Wicksteed, P. H. : *Reactions of Philosophy and Theology.* London, 1920.

V

TE AND WORLD-EMPIRE

NGUISHED authority on political science
med up the Middle Ages in one tremendous
War! The epigram, like most epigrams,
truth for point, but there is enough weight
to make it stick. Certainly he who is but
the mediæval story, and particularly in the
story of that century and that country with which I am here
mainly concerned, is apt to wonder how time or energy
could have been left for any other interest. War seems
the universal occupation—war *in excelsis* of course between
the two mighty opposites of mediævalism, those majestic
figures now almost lost to view in the gathering mists of
time—the Pope and the Emperor—but war also between
Emperor and vassal, between Emperor and commune, between town and town—war between Guelf and Ghibelline,
between black Guelf and white Guelf, between street and
street, almost between house and house—everywhere
turbulence, confusion, anarchy!

Yet if the student will go but a little deeper, will consider
a little more carefully, above all will do that which is so
necessary for all true students of history, but which so
many neglect, and gain at least some elementary acquaintance with the art of the time, there will come upon him a
revulsion of feeling. He will discover that this age of
murder, rapine, and burning, when men seemed only not

107

all the time at one another's throats, was also a period distinguished by an art of a peculiar beauty and a peculiar appeal. It was the time of Giotto's charming frescoes at Padua and in the church of Santa Croce at Florence ; sculpture had recovered something of its Greek glory and its Greek simplicity in the work of Niccola Pisano at Pisa ; above all it was the age of a particularly graceful architecture. And if the student perseveres in his inquiry so that his acquaintance deepens and widens he will be astonished to find that the characteristic of this art is not, as he might expect, horror, grief, disorder, tumult, but a certain gracious serenity, the like of which is found in no other age except in the best days of ancient Greece. Anyone who studies, if only from pictures and photographs, the beautiful angels at Bordeaux, or the cathedral of Amiens, or, in ᚘur own land, the graceful ' Early English ' of Westminster and Salisbury, will understand what I mean. If art is the truest, the deepest, the most significant expression of the real tendencies of the time, of the finer spirit of the age, one surely decides that there is a mistake somewhere and that the first diagnosis is altogether too superficial. The waves were tossing fiercely on the surface, but far down below strong slow currents must have run unseen, making for unity and peace.

Is it to give too free a rein to fancy, for instance, to suggest that he who, in this country at any rate, wishes to understand the spirit of the thirteenth century will gain a truer idea of its meaning if he will sometimes stand in the close at Salisbury and contemplate at leisure, and in silence, the harmonious lines of that most beautiful, most serene, most religious, if I may be allowed the phrase, because most at unity with itself, of all our cathedrals, compact as it is of simplicity and grace, and then turn and turn again the pages of the *Divine Comedy*—than if he is familiar with a whole library of text-books ?

The message of Salisbury is peace, the message of Amiens, of Reims, of Bordeaux is peace ; the teaching of Giotto and Niccola is peace, and no one who will approach their work in a receptive and humble mood can come, I am sure, to any other conclusion.

And, above all, the message of the greatest spirit of the age, of Dante Alighieri, *exul immeritus*—" banished by no fault of his own," *Florentinus natione non moribus*—" Florentine by birth but not by character "—is peace. World-peace was, to use a favourite metaphor of his own, the target at which all his shafts were sped, and it is because in his day he saw no other approach to the desired consummation, that he so ardently advocates world-empire and a world-emperor. To him the empire meant peace, that peace on earth which is the image of the heavenly peace that passes all understanding.

But he is not content simply to assume that peace is a desirable possession for humanity. He will show why it is. He will prove it by his strong logic. He will found it on the testimony of Holy Writ and the teachings of only less holy philosophy. Syllogism by syllogism he will establish it and make both it and the means to attain it clear and convincing for all but those whose hearts are blinded by prejudice and greed. We are apt to smile—when we do not sneer—at Dante's naïve belief in the efficacy of the syllogism. It is a weapon that has fallen into some discredit in modern days. No doubt the mediæval thinker deceived himself when he regarded it as a sure method of discovering the truth ; possibly to found the conduct of life and the governance of the State on self-evident principles, those axioms which are ' perspicuous ' by themselves, is a less sound method than the opportunism of thought and practice of to-day.

Anyhow, we cannot understand mediæval thought unless we realise the domination, the tyranny almost, which the syllogism then exercised over men's minds. The appeal to the syllogism was only less frequent—if it was less frequent—than the appeal to the sword. The syllogism, as M. Janet tells us, was in those days no dead formula, no mere plan or diagram of the mind's workings, but a thing with life and movement and almost a soul of its own. The laws of the syllogism are infallible, just as are the laws of the heavenly bodies. They have to be discovered, but once discovered we cannot think otherwise than in accordance with them.

We will start then, as he starts, with a self-evident truth. " Nothing that is made by God and Nature is superfluous." Dante found the thought in Aristotle. He found it and he reproduced it, but be it noted that he uses the singular verb. Literally it runs, "God and Nature *makes* nothing superfluous "—for Nature is but the hand of God. In other words, anything created by God, through the operation of Nature, His mighty instrument, has some distinct purpose to serve. More than that, to whatever attribute is possessed by any being whatever there is assured by God's providence a corresponding good. Dante had no firmer conviction than this. Listen to part of the dialogue between Carlo Martello and himself in the heaven of Venus. Carlo Martello is speaking :

" 'Wherefore whatever this bow discharges falls disposed to a foreseen end, just as a thing aimed right upon its mark. If this were not so the heavens where thou journeyest would so produce their effect that they would not be an artist's work but ruins. And this cannot be, if the intellects which move these stars are not maimed, and maimed the First, in that he has not perfected them. Wilt thou that this truth dawn more upon thee ? ' And I : ' No longer, because I see it is impossible for Nature in that which is necessary to fail.' " [1]

The world is not a ruin. God is not like the human artist who " has the habit of his art, but a hand that trembles." So we start with our major premiss. The minor follows : " God and Nature ' has ' created man." And so we reach the inevitable conclusion that man is created for some end. His life is not, or is not meant to be, a mere race to death.

What then are we to conclude is the end for which man was created ? Now we know another thing. We are certain that man was not created to live alone. He is a gregarious animal, a creature formed to live in society, in communion with his fellow men. This being the case, we must not consider the individual man, but try to discover the end of man in general—humanity. For what purpose was human society created ? What, in Dante's own phrase, is the ultimate goal for which eternal God by His art, which is Nature, brings into being the human race in its entirety ? Or, to put it more concisely, what is the goal of civilisation ?

In order to get at the answer let us compare and contrast man with the other creations of God. What attribute, what quality differentiates man from other creatures ? We will proceed by a method of elimination. Obviously it is not ' being,' not mere existence. *That* he shares with all the elements. Not ' organised being,' which is to be found also in the minerals. Not ' animated being,' which

[1] Passages quoted from the *Divine Comedy* are taken from Butler's translation.

the plants likewise possess. Not ' sensation,' because this is shared by the brutes, but "apprehension by means of the potential intellect," for this gift is bestowed by God on no other creature above or below.

What do we mean by a ' potential intellect ' ? The words and the idea came to mediæval thinkers through the great Arabian commentator on Aristotle whom we know by the name of Averroës. It means a mind, a power of understanding, an intellect which is capable of far more than it achieves at any one given moment. " Ah," says Robert Browning,

> Ah, but a man's reach should exceed his grasp,
> Or what's a heaven for ?

That is it exactly :

> A *man's* reach should exceed his grasp.

That is what Dante meant and mediæval thought under-stood :

> A man's reach *should* exceed his grasp.

A brute's reach, a plant's reach, a mineral's reach is equated, so to speak, with its grasp. Each in its own limited range performs its perfect work and is satisfied. It can go no farther—in a sense it desires to go no farther. It reaches its goal. That is, it has no free will. I will not stop to criticise this position; I will simply state it as a pre-supposition of mediæval psychology. But man can always do more than he does. That is his privilege—and also his tragedy. He has free will. He has the potential intellect, and this potential intellect cannot be always actualised by one man, or any limited association of men. That accounts for multiplicity.

There must be multiplicity for the actualisation of man's ends. The work then for the human race, taken in its totality, is to keep in activity the whole power of the potential intellect, primarily for speculation and secondarily—by extension and for the sake of speculation—for action. Primarily, be it noted, for speculation. Dante is faithful to Aristotle in this, as in so much besides.

But is he faithful to the truth also? Is he right in saying, as he goes on to say, that in sitting still and in quietness the particular man is made perfect, and that therefore in the tranquillity of peace the human race is most freely and easily disposed to its proper task?

Action exists for the sake of speculation—or shall we call it contemplation? Is not this the humour of the philosopher, of the student remote from affairs? Peace is obviously necessary for contemplation, but are we to regard the contemplative life as the most desirable? Many would deny it. They think of the contemplative life as lazy, unpractical, useless. But are we so certain that Aristotle and the mediævalists were wrong? Rightly considered, all man's strivings, whether for wealth or power or what not, are in the last analysis that he may lead the good life, as he understands it, and in order to live it he must understand it, and in order to understand it he must contemplate it, and the power of contemplation once reached he may find not only that he leads no lazy, selfish existence, but that—dare it be said?—he is not far from what Christ meant by the Kingdom of Heaven. I confess that I myself cannot otherwise explain activity. Or is activity for activity's sake—a sort of squirrel-like running round and round in a cage more or less gilded—the desirable life? Anyhow, granted that the purpose for which the human race is created is to unfold the infinite riches of the human mind, the conclusion comes with almost irresistible power. If it is to make active all the latent possibilities there must obviously be, before that actualisation can take place, one condition, and that condition can be none other than universal peace. Universal peace is the best of all those things which were ordained for our beatitude. And that is why the message that rang out to the shepherds was not riches, not pleasure, not honour, not length of life, not health, not strength, not beauty, but peace. "Glory to God in the highest, and on earth peace to men of goodwill." Surely there is no necessity for Dante to marshal before us a legion of arguments to prove a truth so sun-clear as the necessity for peace. We need no Aristotle or Averroës, with their potential and actual intellects, come from the grave to tell us this !

I would answer, first of all, that it is no bad thing that if we desire peace we should think out clearly why we desire it. It may be that the reason why peace is such a rare visitant to this planet is that we have never understood how to treat her when she comes. Secondly, we have to remember that at the time Dante was writing the mediæval mind drew all its principles from two sources and two sources only—the teachings of the Church, and the principles of Aristotle. They were the moulds into which mediæval thought was naturally poured.

But let us not be too hasty in our condemnation of the mediævalists. For though the mould gives shape to that which runs into it the mould does not create its contents. The principles were Aristotelian and scriptural, but the thought was not, or at any rate not always. We ought not to imagine that because Aristotle is quoted with tiresome iteration therefore the movement of the mediæval mind was, so to speak, frozen at the source. Man at any time and in any conditions, even in our own most enlightened days, usually finds that for which he is looking. The mediæval

thinkers found warrant for their conclusions in Aristotle.
His authority was compelling, and no doubt it is true
that the mediævalists were often bondslaves to the letter.
I suppose it would not be quite fair to suggest that much
modern thought is conditioned by the categories supplied
ready-made by Newton and Darwin. The parallel is,
I know, not quite exact, but I am a little inclined to think
that future ages may make our dependence on these great
names something of a reproach, if not a scandal. Indeed,
has not the reproach already begun ? We have heard of
Einstein ! It is certain at any rate that many doctrines
were found in Aristotle which that philosopher would
have heartily repudiated. The scholars and poets of the
Middle Ages were not exact critics. They took their
own where they found it, but it was sometimes their own
that they took. Man's spirit was not so tightly cabined
as we are sometimes led to suppose. Even a superficial
acquaintance with the literature of the thirteenth and
fourteenth centuries discovers not a few flagrant heresies
in belief, many instances of thought that pushed out
adventurously into the most unfamiliar and least charted
seas, of speculation that denied the most cherished and most
authoritative dogmas—nay, sometimes scaled and almost
shook the very seat of the omnipotent. I doubt, for
instance, if in the whole course of history, from that time
to this, any court of any sovereign was more free-thinking
and more enlightened than that of the second Frederick
and of his son Manfred. And it is interesting to note
that though the stern and loyal churchman in Dante
meted out to the Emperor the deadly doom of those who
deny the soul's immortality we cannot but feel that he
seizes with avidity on the slenderest excuse for getting
Manfred, in defiance of the ban of the Church and the

express ordinance of the Vicar of God, out of the torments of Hell and into the milder climate of Purgatory.

Anyhow, if we are to attain to this felicity, this opportunity to enjoy our peculiar inheritance as man, to actualise the potential intellect, the one thing needful is unity, for mankind with all its myriad divisions is really one. And if unity of aim, then, as it seemed to Dante, unity of direction.

Consider the individual man. What is it that promotes his happiness most surely? We know, all of us, that it is only when all our powers, all our purposes, all our strivings, are controlled and harmonised by reason—by the intellectual faculty. If the kingdom be divided against itself it cannot stand. In a family the goal of which is the good life of the individual members there must be one ultimate will to which all disputes must in the last instance be referred. And so for the whole human race, ordained, as we have found it is ordained, for a single end, there must surely be one guiding and controlling power—below, that is, the supreme power "whose will is our peace." Otherwise the end cannot be secured. And that guiding and controlling power is exactly what we mean, in Dante's opinion, when we talk of 'monarch'—by derivation 'sole ruler'—or, to use the more familiar term, 'emperor.' It is proved therefore that for the well-being of the world there must be empire.

But further proofs are added. Let us start from any whole—for mediæval thought always starts from the whole —and then consider the meaning of the parts. The parts obviously exist first for the sake of the whole. Otherwise it would be no whole but a meaningless heap of fragments. Again, let us note how in order to further organised and civilised life man constantly creates and as constantly destroys institutions. Does the institution exist primarily for its own good ? Is it not the very vice of institutions that they so often think, if the expression be permitted, first of their own good and only secondly of the purpose for which they were instituted ?

And so it is obvious that all the various institutions of society must be ordered with reference to the kingdom of which they form a part, and all the kingdoms in turn with reference to a single kingdom and a single ruler—that is, in other words, the monarch : or, better, the monarchy. Note that addition—" or monarchy." The idea that it is not the official in himself that matters but the office, or function, for which that official was appointed, is implied in all Dante's thinking. The actual holder of the office is a man and therefore liable to err, and he does err in a multitude of ways. For the office Dante has a great reverence, for the holders none whatever. He is, indeed, no respecter of persons. Hardly any sin was greater in his eyes than the neglect of high office by its holder. Students of the *Comedy* will recall many instances. Witness the bitter reproaches launched against " Albert the German " for neglecting Italy, " the garden of the Empire " ! Witness the disappointment breathing in every line when the stately figure is described who in the valley of the kings in the *Purgatorio* " sits highest and has the semblance of having neglected that which he ought to have done— Rudolf the Emperor who had the power to heal the wounds which have slain Italy " ! Witness above all the awful doom to which even individual Vicars of God are consigned because they neglected their duties, or regarded their office as an opportunity for private gain, for self-seeking ! There rises to one's mind the great passage in the *Paradiso* when the Apostle Peter, a very flame, grows redder and redder, while the whole heaven, in sympathy, is overspread with the hue of sunset, as he denounces the man that " usurps on earth my place, my place, my place " (how damning the effect of the threefold iteration !), " which is vacant in the sight of the Son of God, and has of my burying-place made a sewer of the blood and filth wherewith the perverse one, who fell from this place on high, down there is appeased."

And again, the office and the officer exist not for the sake of the ruler but of the ruled. The Emperor, like the Pope, is properly considered *servus servorum*—the servant of servants. So when Dante speaks of the Emperor or monarch it must be realised that he is thinking of no individual Otto or Frederick but the ideal Emperor—the Emperor as he ought to be—the veritable Messiah almost, for whom he was so constantly and so vainly looking—the *dux*, the *veltro*—who should chase the wolf of avarice and greed back to the place whence envy first sent her forth. So sublime is his ideal of the real Emperor who should faithfully discharge his high office that when at long last, after many disappointments, one holder of the Imperial sceptre, Henry of Luxembourg, did actually show himself eager to enter on his real inheritance, and assert himself as the veritable successor of the Cæsars of old, Dante gratefully assigns to him by anticipation a place in the yellow of the everlasting rose of Paradise. " Look how great is the assembly of the white garments," cries the heavenly guide. " Behold our city, how great is its circuit ! Behold there our stalls so full, that few folk hereafter are awaited. In that great seat on which thou hast thine eyes by reason of the crown which already is placed over it, ere thou shalt sup at this wedding-feast will sit the soul, which on earth shall be imperial, of the high Henry who will come to set Italy straight before that she shall be ready."

Indeed, one may say that it is never the Emperor, the person, of whom he is thinking but something much more abstract, far more typical. It is Law, personified ; Law, throned and crowned, and invested with majesty and honour. The person is but the living, the temporal, embodiment of the eternal law and everlasting order. And we must never forget here that to all thinkers of that age Law was not, as we are apt to regard it now, the result of the slow growth, the tardy ripening, of a many-centuried harvest of custom after custom, of precedent on precedent, but a truth always there waiting to be discovered. It was, as Professor Jenks puts it, the expression by the wisdom of the age of that reason which men were coming more and more to look upon as the true index to the will of the unseen power. To Rome of old time it had been divinely revealed. This belief was held just as firmly as the other belief that the gospel had been divinely revealed to the Jews.

Again, the universe is a unity—the very name shows it. And God is pre-eminently one, and God made man in His own image, and therefore man, in order to realise his perfection, must resemble God as far as he can. When the pilgrim from time to eternity has ascended under the guidance of the blessed Beatrice, who typifies the illumination from on high, to the ninth heaven—the heaven of the fixed stars—he sees a point "which radiated light so keen that the sight, which it fires, must needs close itself for the great keenness," and Beatrice explains to him in Aristotelian phrase again that "from that point depends the heaven and all nature."

And so earthly power will then show most like God's

when in a similar way all thrones and principalities and powers depend on one. The celestial hierarchy is to be in all points the pattern and model of that which is below. Man, moreover, is the son of heaven, begotten—according to an illustration also from his master, and quaintly misunderstood—" by man and the sun." For just as, according to the astrology of the time, the whole heaven was regulated by a single motion, the *primum mobile*, and a single mover, God, so the human race is best disposed when ruled by a single prince—that is, a single mover, and by a single law—that is, a single movement.

Again, we know that in this world, so rude and so imperfect an image of the perfection of its Creator, contentions do and must arise. But, as the great Augustine says in a passage that was evidently familiar to Dante, all contention, all struggle, all war levels at peace. Peace is the goal of all fighting. But whose peace—mine or yours ? Who is to decide ? Again we see the necessity for a supreme tribunal and a supreme prince to hold the scales.

Obviously Dante is not thinking of a super-state, the supremacy of one nation over others : certainly not Italy ' over all,' for of course the Empire was German, but the existence of a supreme law to hold all national ideals, passions, animosities in check. And the other name for this supreme law can be nothing else than Justice. But we know by experience that Justice rarely holds her sway unbiassed and unaffected by personal greed, the ambition of individuals, the passions incident to humanity. And Justice, moreover, consists in rendering to each man his due. It is a virtue that essentially refers to others. What man is capable of it ? And here comes the tremendous assumption. There is or can be just one person unswayed by passion, undisturbed by ambition and greed. And that

person is the monarch—the Emperor ! And why ?
Because being everything, having all, he has nothing
left him to desire. The possessions of all lower princes
are bounded by those of others, but his jurisdiction is
terminated by the all-embracing ocean alone.

The assertion leaves one breathless. There seems something seriously amiss with the psychology. By that sin fell the
angels. All history seems against him here. And indeed,
as critics have not been slow to point out, we have one
striking instance to falsify his contention. Alexander, rapidly
approaching, as he thought, the conquest of the whole
civilised world, sighs that he will soon have no worlds to
conquer ! Certainly the pattern of such an Empire and
such an Emperor is laid up in heaven, but then, Dante
would rejoin, that is exactly where it should be laid up.
Man has but to search for it and he will find it, and finding
it can realise it on earth. Did he know, we are permitted
to wonder, the reasoned conviction of another and a greater
thinker that the world would never be properly governed
till philosophers were kings, or kings philosophers ?

But other-earthly, remote from the real affairs of men as
seems this vision, there yet runs a strong current of common
sense through his loftiest imaginings. The supreme ruler
can have no rival near the throne, yet he cannot of course
be constantly interfering in local affairs. The human race
must be ruled by him and guided by his common rule
to peace. He gives the general direction : particular
princes must carry out the particular decisions just as—
note the simile—the practical intellect receives the major
proposition from the speculative intellect and adds under
it the particular proposition which is properly its own,
and so proceeds to the practical conclusion. But all must
flow from one, exactly as all in nature does flow from One,

so that all confusion concerning universal principles may be removed.

And let us consider when the birth of Him who was by essence and title the Prince of Peace took place. If we search the records of human history from the fall right onward to the present time there was never any period when the world had universal peace except in the reign of Augustus, when there was a perfect monarchy. And that peaceful rule of that perfect monarch was awaited by the Son of God, when about to become man for man's salvation.

There does exist then on earth already—we have not to wait for its manifestation—an authority to which can safely be committed this tremendous task—the Roman Emperor and the Roman Empire. It is true that the nations have raged against it and the people imagined vain things. Dante himself had at one time qualms about its justice and a doubt whether its power had not been acquired rather by force than righteousness. And as that, I think, would naturally be the first conclusion of the ordinary student, it is interesting to follow in the track of Dante's thought and see how so powerful and acute a mind could persuade itself that the Roman Empire was the divinely appointed instrument for its purpose. And here too we will start with an assumption, a self-evident truth, a major premiss. Whatever God wills in the society of men is to be regarded as true and pure right. But of course the difficulty is to be certain how we shall know God's will. It is in itself invisible to men, but the invisible things of God are perceived by the things which are made. Even a man's will is only perceived, save to the man himself, by signs. It is a question of rightly discerning the signs; it is again a matter of argument, of syllogism, of reading and interpreting evidence. Now it is meet that the noblest people should be set above all others. But that the Roman people were the noblest is obvious by most certain proofs. Their founder was Æneas, and Virgil tells us that none was "more just through piety or greater by force and arms."

It is proved by the founder's inheritance, through three ancestors, of three continents. It is proved—marvellous to relate !—by his three marriages, which also carried with them rights over three continents. Creusa, his first wife, was a Trojan from Asia; his second wife, Lavinia, an Italian—a European ; and then—and here even the most judicious will grieve, if they do not smile—by a most perverse, if most charitable mistranslation of a line in Virgil,

Conjugium vocat, hoc prætexit nomine culpam,[1]

his third 'wife,' Dido, whom, we remember, he left, and many readers, forgetting Jove's high decree, never forgive him for leaving, on the fatal shore, sorrowing and planning the last resource of the forsaken—Dido brought with her Africa as her dower !

One would wonder to what class of readers such arguments could have been addressed did not one know that they were almost the commonplaces of the political controversies of the day. Each age interprets and reinterprets and misinterprets history after its own fashion, and each age will find in history what it most desires to find. Before the eyes of the most painstaking, the most conscientious, historian a mist is spread which he can never wholly dissipate, the mist of his own prejudices and prepossessions. But the mist here is surely more opaque than usual ! One may be forgiven for imagining the gracious ghost of Virgil somewhere in the Elysian fields feeling perhaps a trifle

[1] Literally, "She calls it wedlock—behind this name she screens her sin."

uncomfortable at his words being understood in quite so
strange a fashion.

And other arguments follow just as amazing to modern
ears. It would be wearisome, as it is needless, to recount
them in detail. We shall become conscious in reading
them that far more water has flowed under the bridges of
Tiber and of Thames than we had supposed. It is not
only that Dante accepts without the least demur all that is
written in the *Æneid*, as he does all that Livy, the professional historian, has stated in his chronicles, that he believes
implicitly in the picturesque legends of early Rome, the
miracles that are to him as true and as divinely produced
as the miracles of Christianity. He is perfectly convinced
also that the Romans constantly acted in all their deeds
and all their conquests in a strong and unselfish public
spirit, that they contemplated the goal of right and justice
not *per accidens* but *per essentiam*, that they willed the end as
well as the means. It was no chance that brought them
to their divinely appointed goal. To Dante the title-deeds
of the Romans to a divine commission could be as clearly
read as the title-deeds of the other chosen people of God.
And when all else is doubtful and all other expedients have
been tried, the judgment of God can rightly be invoked
and clearly revealed by single combat, and by a series of
single combats the Romans entered on their imperial career!
Just as to the Jews it was assigned by the inscrutable
decrees of the divine providence that in the fulness of time
they should be the appointed vessel for the conveyance of
the gospel, so to the Romans it was ordained that they
should be revealers, under God, of law and order and justice to
mankind. This duality, this twofold destiny for mankind,
is a faith held by Dante with the most complete sincerity
and conviction. For the Jews the gospel, for the Romans

the law—the latter a divine revelation differing in degree. indeed, but not differing in kind, from the greater revelation of the gospel. Man being a creature of two worlds has need of two revelations, one for earthly blessedness, the other for the blessedness of eternity. This being so, Nature *must* have ordained a place and a people for universal command, else she would have been wanting to herself— which by hypothesis is impossible. " It is impossible," you remember, " for Nature in that which is necessary to fail." And of what other people than the Romans can fitness for universal command be predicted? Witness the great lines :

> Tu regere imperio populos Romane memento,
> Hæ tibi erunt artes pacisque imponere morem,
> Parcere subjectis et debellare superbos.

How deep was the impression made upon the sensitive poetic mind of Dante by the *Æneid* is apparent in the whole treatment of his theme. It had been Virgil's mission to impress upon the Romans that they were a peculiar people, chosen by the counsels of the most High to fulfil, after heroic struggles, a mighty purpose :

> Tantæ molis erat Romanam condere gentem.

And so potent was the spell he wove that even in the eclipse of learning which followed the barbarian anarchy and the Lombard gloom the study of Virgil never wholly disappeared from the land. Strange, uncouth figures had for many generations flitted in a sort of wild phantasmagoria across the stage in that Rome for which he prophesied so great a destiny. The Cæsars had deserted their inherit- ance ; a strange new cult from the barbaric East had pos- sessed itself of men's minds ; the Vestal Virgins had departed for ever, and the sacred flame was quenched ; yet the *Æneid* lived on to fire the genius of a still mightier

poet, and so to thrill him with its beauty and its teaching
that a hand was stretched out across the ages and the
Christian with a childlike faith followed the pagan up to
the very verge and confines of eternity.

Surely this is one of the most wonderful things in history.
We know that by some strange fate Virgil in the Middle
Ages was regarded as more magician than poet. Was ever
greater magic wrought than this, and did ever poet meet
so long after his death with a fate so beautiful ? *Habent
sua fata libelli* indeed! There is quoted in the second
book of the *De Monarchia*—Dante's great political treatise—
a saying the origin of which no scholar has yet been able
to discover, but which at any rate goes back to times long
anterior to Dante's age. *Romanum Imperium nascitur
de fonte pietatis*—" The Roman Empire springs from the
fount of compassion." Had it been Dante's own, I should
have been tempted to conjecture that he drew the idea
straight from reading and rereading the *Æneid*, from a
memory of some of those lines or half-lines that are among
the most pregnant and poignant things in literature, the
Sunt lacrimæ rerum, the tears that rise for man and his
mortality ; the *Dis aliter visum* of the plangent lament for
the young Marcellus ; or the moving episode of Dido's
death, or a hundred others. Certainly one does not
usually associate the quality of mercy with the Roman rule.
The *Delenda est Carthago*, the Tullianum, and the slave-
market rise up in judgment against them. So far as any
generalisation about a people can be true, it is true, I think,
that the Roman temper was a hard temper, its spirit an
austere spirit. It was, as their religion shows, legalist
through and through, and legalism rarely leans to mercy.
And to the mind of the student, trained in the classics,
there inevitably rises up the memory of another and more

famous epigram—the caustic phrase with which the historian of the early Empire sears the laurels of the conquering race : *Solitudinem faciunt, pacem appellant*—" They make a solitude and call it peace." Dante, it is certain, never knew the works of Tacitus. Would it have made any difference to his judgment of Roman history had he read them ? The question is perhaps idle ; anyhow, it is easily answered. He knew well and constantly quotes from Lucan, a republican like Tacitus, as convinced and as severe, whose sounding rhetoric is only less effective because more academic and less sincere, when he denounces the works of imperialism. He knew Lucan, and through knowing him he is guilty of one of those strange lapses from consistency which occasionally surprise and shock one in the reading of his poem. Cato, the stern uncompromising republican, the hater of absolutism, who chose to die by his own hand rather than see the destruction of the liberty which he worshipped, is given the very highest dignity that, except by a special miracle, one who lived before the time of Christ could receive at Dante's hands. He is the warder at the very entrance to Purgatory. And yet in the lowest depths of Hell, where Lucifer, " the emperor of the realm of woe," stands sunk in ice, on each side of the arch-traitor Judas, who betrayed his divine Master, are tortured the betrayers of their imperial lord, the tyrannicides Brutus and Cassius. And their tortures, moreover, are of such a kind that even the genius of Dante cannot prevent us from feeling them to be impossibly revolting and grotesque.

So true it is again that even the sincere thinker takes from his history mainly what suits his purpose. To rend the Empire is with Dante another rending of the seamless garment. But "the Roman Empire springs from the fount of compassion"! Did ever imperialism receive so splendid a testimonial from a source so noble?

Certainly to Dante, if the Middle Ages were war, the Empire meant peace. "There went forth a decree from Cæsar Augustus that all the world should be enrolled!" One seems to hear in the very roll and rhythm of the sentence the tramp of the imperial legions to do their master's bidding—the pomp and power and majesty of *Imperator Romanus.*

"There went forth a decree." The scripture has said it! Unquestioning obedience to a divinely-given command is implicit in every word of the text. "There went forth a decree," and whosoever voluntarily obeys such a decree obviously gives sanction to its justice. Christ Himself obeyed the decree. What further need have we of witnesses?

And then follows the great strange argument which, so far as the commentators are aware, is entirely original. Christ voluntarily took upon Himself a human nature, and with that human nature took also that sin of Adam wherein all mankind had sinned. Therefore, in so far as it was human nature that was punished in Christ, the sentence was incontestably just, pronounced by a duly authorised official, by Pilate the accredited representative of Tiberius, the Roman Emperor. Christ by consenting to the sentence sealed for ever by His blood His acceptance of the sovereign authority of the Empire. In such wise the divine drama was played out: such is the teaching of the heavenly allegory!

Two questions may now be presumed to be settled: one, that there must be supreme rule; the other, that the title to the supreme rule inheres in the Roman people.

But here a difficulty arises. Who were the Roman

people? Not certainly the Italians of the day; there was no Italy except geographically. And long since the secret of Empire had been divulged, that an Emperor could be created elsewhere than at Rome. And not only the Emperor but the Empire! The Empire had been translated; neither Roman nor Græco-Roman, it was now German. I do not think Dante ever really addresses himself to this difficulty. He seems to be positing an ideal people just as he cried for an ideal Emperor. Or was it his opinion that since the grave burghers of the old Roman commonwealth had discovered God's purpose of empire it mattered little whence or how the ruler came—God would provide? There were the electors truly, but their business was not to choose but to announce the choice. They were to be the heralds of the divine providence. However we take it, we must admit, I think, a serious lacuna in the logic. Did he believe in a sort of apostolical succession of peoples?

And above and beyond all this there is a formidable lion in his path, the tremendous figure of the Pope—and such a Pope: a Boniface VIII mitred and throned, claiming *both* swords and with a more formidable weapon still in his hand, the bull *Unam Sanctam*, while from his lips issues the thrasonical utterance, "I am Cæsar, I am Emperor"—he, God's own Vicar, the successor of Peter, who in very truth bears the keys of the Kingdom of Heaven. For surely the long procession of arguments by which has been established the necessity for unity of direction has established also the conviction that the successor of the Cæsars is none other than he who possesses the inheritance of the Cæsars and is seated in their ancient capital—the Roman Pontiff.

Admitted even the necessity for an Emperor as well as

I

a Pontiff, the former stands to the latter as the moon to the sun, shining but by a borrowed light and dependent for all light and all glory on the other. Just as God created two great luminaries, the one to rule the day and the other to rule the night—the smaller being inferior to and dependent on the former—so there may be on earth two vicars of his providence, but the earthly one must in all things be subject to him who derives his title directly from heaven. Against Dante's contention likewise is the whole weight of the authority of the decretalists, the exponents of ecclesiastical law. Against him is every analogy—and arguments from analogy were of great authority in those days—drawn from nature, from scripture, and from history generally.

From scripture, when the disciples said, " Lord, behold, here are two swords," did not Christ reply, as seeming to acquiesce, " It is enough " ? Again, Levi, who typifies the Church, was the elder son : Judah, the type of the Empire, the younger. Did not also Samuel, the heavenly prophet, expressly take away the kingdom from Saul, the earthly monarch, and bestow it on another ?

From history two facts, for facts in Dante's eyes they are : first, the Donation of Constantine, that extraordinary forgery of some subtle and unscrupulous clerk of earlier date—the grant of liberty and lordship to Holy Church, and the relinquishment to the successor of Peter, with the Emperor's withdrawal from Rome, of all power and property in the West ; second, the conferment of the dignity of Emperor, when the Empire was translated from Greek to Frank, by the Pope upon Charles the Great.

I can only summarise very shortly the subtle but not particularly profound arguments which Dante employs against these contentions. He had not been trained in rhetoric for nothing. He turns the weapons of his opponents against themselves. It is ridiculous to suppose that God created the sun and the moon as heavenly exemplars of the papal and Imperial powers. The very fact that these two great luminaries were created on the fourth day, whereas man was only created on the sixth day, shows that God had no such intention. One does not provide for what is not yet existent! Moreover, even if He had, it is still to be noted that the moon has her own proper motion and her own proper mover (the angel, in the astrology of the day, that moves her sphere) and her own proper rays. She is by no means entirely dependent on the sun. And as to the argument from Levi and Judah, if Levi was the elder this does not imply his authority over Judah; one may be elder in years and yet inferior in authority.

As for the argument of the two swords, one must get behind mere words—one wishes that Dante had done this in other parts of his argument!—and seek out the *intention* of Christ, whose Kingdom, as He expressly states, is not of this world. As for Samuel, his commission was a temporary one—*ad hoc*, so to speak.

As for Constantine and his Donation, it is perfectly clear that no man by virtue of his office can do that which is counter to that office, or obviously the office would quickly be null and void. For the Emperor to rend the Empire is a contradiction in terms. He cannot do it! And it is to rend that seamless tunic anew which even *they* dared not do who pierced Christ, very God, with a lance. Again, the Empire as well as the Church has its own foundation. The latter is founded on Christ, the former on human right, and the Empire no more than the Church can do anything contrary to its own foundation. Moreover, every jurisdiction is prior to its judge; the judge is appointed to the jurisdiction, and not conversely. And if one Emperor could do what Constantine did so could another, and so on *ad infinitum*. As to the argument about Charles, that proves nothing or proves too much. If one Pope conferred the dignity on Charles, on the other hand the Emperor Otto deposed another Pope, Benedict, and appointed a Leo in his place. And a clinching argument against the authority of the Church being the source of the imperial authority is that before the Church, humanly speaking, was existent, the Empire was exercising its full and proper excellence.

Again, both Christ and the Church sanction the Empire, the Christ by His birth and death, the Church when Paul appealed to Cæsar. And above all, the nature of the Church is the form of the Church, and the form of the Church is the life of Christ, who said, " My Kingdom is not of this world "—not of course, Dante hastens to add, that the whole round world and all that therein is do not belong to Christ as God, but that as exemplar of the Church He has no charge over this kingdom.

And here suddenly the logician leaves his desk ; the poet, the seer, takes up the argument. We stand on higher ground. We are conscious of a different atmosphere altogether.

Man by the very law of his nature holds a place midway between the corruptible and the incorruptible ; he is likened to the horizon between two hemispheres. Consider him as a physical body, he is corruptible ; but consider him from the point of view of the soul—the soul admits not of corruption and decay. Again, to change the metaphor, he is the mean between two extremes. Now a mean must partake of the nature of each of the two extremes of which it is a mean.

Again, as we have already shown, every nature is ordained

to a proper end.　Man, therefore, having a twofold nature must have a twofold end—one corruptible, the other incorruptible.　And before this mortal puts on immortality, before, in Dante's own phrase, the caterpillar that man is changes to the angelic butterfly that he is to be, he must attain to the blessedness of this, his mortal life.　Now the blessedness of this life consists in the full, perfect, and unhampered exercise of his particular powers, those powers to which we have already referred.　This position is typified by the terrestrial Paradise, the Garden of Eden which man once inhabited, but which, by the sin of Adam, he had forfeited.　Therefore the one essential task he has to perform is, by all means, to get back to the terrestrial Paradise. It will be remembered how Dante, the typical man, achieves this indispensable labour in the *Divine Comedy*.　Virgil has been his guide through the valley of Hell, and up the steep slope of Purgatory, but when the Garden of Eden is reached again, Virgil, to the intense, bitter grief of his disciple, disappears.　He has performed his work ; he has directed his charge back to the crown and summit of his earthly life.　He vanishes, and his place when the pilgrim is now pure and disposed to see the everlasting stars is taken by Beatrice—the true light of God.　For to these two ends, as diverse, man must come by diverse means ; to one by the teaching of human philosophy, as typified again by Virgil, to the other by spiritual teaching according to the three theological virtues, faith, hope, and charity, and for this task no purely human teacher, be he even as great as Virgil, can suffice.

And though these ends are made plain by human reason and by the Holy Spirit, yet human greed would, for mere temporal enjoyment, cast them on one side were man not held in sway by bit and rein.　And it is the task of the

Emperor to insert that bit and guide that rein. So, in conclusion, man has need of a twofold direction, from the High Pontiff to lead him to eternal life, from the Emperor to attain, through him and in accordance with philosophy's teachings, all the felicity that time could give.

Were man as pure and innocent as in his stainless prime, new-minted from the hands of God, he would need neither the one nor the other. So, when Dante, the typical man once more, has finished his pilgrimage through the realm of woe and the healing penances of Purgatory, and is ready for the flight to the stars, he is told that he needs no more direction. Over himself he is now both crowned and mitred. Man unfallen in a perfect world would be his own Pope and his own Emperor. But man has fallen, and so God out of His infinite goodness and consideration for his fallen state has arranged for both powers.

It is the Emperor's business to see that on this threshing-floor of mortality life shall be lived in freedom and peace. And the Emperor, be it understood, is as divinely chosen as the Pope. The electors who nominally choose him are but the announcers of the divine will. But all the same Cæsar must observe the reverence to Peter which a first-born son owes to his father, so that, illuminated by the light of paternal peace, he may with greater power illuminate the world.

Such is the crowning argument. The demonstration is concluded. It is not necessary for me to point out, as indeed I have hinted once or twice in the course of this chapter, how thin and unsubstantial, how puerile, indeed, to modern ears, are many of the arguments employed. The man is so much greater than his arguments. Most men are ! The fact is, I suppose, the strong conviction, due to the man's very nature, to his whole outlook on life, which depends, it may be, on circumstances unknown to the man himself—heredity possibly, early experience, training, temperament, what not—is there before the arguments are considered; they are reinforcements summoned when the position is attacked. This fact does not necessarily vitiate the conclusions. Some of the world's noblest causes rest on the flimsiest foundation of argument. So a man falls in love, and gives a thousand reasons why he fell in love with the one person, and in all probability no single reason is correct. Can we take Dante's position, Dante's belief, strip it of that which is accidental, temporal, insecure, and see if there lies below it any permanent and enduring foundation?

A great scholar, lately lost to us—Lord Bryce—has called the *De Monarchia* rather an epitaph than a prophecy. And in a sense that judgment is true, and in a sense it is false. Considered from the point of view of his own day and the day that followed, no conclusion was more thoroughly and utterly disproved by the facts of history than Dante's pronouncement for a world-empire and a world-emperor. Even as he wrote there were rising, all unseen and unnoticed even by so acute a thinker and so keen-sighted an observer as Dante, great forces which were destined to undermine with increasing rapidity the foundations of the Empire in which he so devoutly believed and to sweep it finally into nothingness. The strong centralised kingdoms of the West were rising in judgment against the Cæsar and against his Empire, and reducing him and it to greater and greater impotence, so that the very implication of the word ' empire ' was by a later generation completely misunderstood, and an adventurer could arrogate to himself a title which took all meaning from the name, and, later still, Europe saw without sense of incongruity three or four emperors when by the very logic of history there could be but one.

But in another and a truer sense I am not so sure of the propriety of ' epitaph.'

Let us not forget, as I have tried to show throughout, that what Dante had in mind was not the Empire or the Emperor *simpliciter*—as such—but some strong central controlling power which could keep human greed and ambition in check, and give to the world that peace which was so necessary for the perfecting of humanity's precious and peculiar gift. Nationalism has, no doubt, brought many good things. It has promoted the internal development — anyhow the material development — of nations and, to a certain extent, kept the peace within their own borders. But to the world at large it has not brought peace but other things, and among them the high explosive and the poisonous gas. We ourselves of this disillusioned generation have learnt by much bitter experience the meaning and the message of nationalism.

Once again the world, or the greater part of it, seems ready—as perhaps never before in the whole history of this tortured planet—to try any means, if means can be found, for promoting that world-peace, " the best of all those things which are ordained for our beatitude." Dante's own solution mankind has rejected, and rejected decisively, and, so far as the expression can be used in this transitory world, ' for ever.' Whether we can adopt the spirit of his contention, while the letter is neglected, is the immediate problem confronting the state-craft of to-day. It is possible that his political vision, blurred as it is by the limitations of his time and his place, may help us to see that, in the words of a victim of the late war, " patriotism is not enough," and with him to catch a glimpse, far away in the distance, of at least the turrets of the true city, which for the better safeguarding of this terrestrial life we shall surely build not on the shifting sands of nationalism, but on the more enduring foundations of international law, international agreement, and—greater than these two things —international sympathy.

E. Sharwood Smith

BIBLIOGRAPHY

A. Primary Sources

Dante Alighieri : Opere.   Ed. Moore.   Oxford, 1904.
Dante Alighieri : Le Opere Latine.   Ed. Giuliani.   Florence, 1878.

Note.—The best translation of the *Divine Comedy* for English readers is probably that of A. J. Butler, 3 vols., Macmillan, 1885–92.   There is also a convenient edition of the whole of Dante's works published by Dent in the Temple Classics series, with the Italian and English facing one another on opposite pages.   In this edition the *De Monarchia* is translated from the Latin original, with the addition of excellent notes, by Philip H. Wicksteed.   There is also a translation of the *De Monarchia* by the late Dean Church which is now out of print.   It is unnecessary to refer to the numerous other translations of the *Divine Comedy*, but it should be understood that the best commentary on Dante's political treatise the *De Monarchia* is furnished by the poet himself in his *Comedy* and in his philosophical treatise *The Convito*, especially Book IV, ch. iv–v.   Some acquaintance with Aristotle's ideas is also desirable, and a useful little book on this subject is Wallace's *Outlines of the Philosophy of Aristotle* (Cambridge, 1908).

B. Secondary Sources

Bryce, Viscount : *Holy Roman Empire.*   Macmillan, 1904.
Church, A. J. : *Dante, and other Essays.*   Macmillan, 1901.
Dante : *De Monarchia.*   With an introduction on the political theory of Dante by W. H. V. Reade.   Oxford, 1916.
Fisher, Herbert : *The Medieval Empire.*   2 vols.   Macmillan, 1898.
Gierke, O. : *Political Theories of the Middle Age.*   Translated by F. W. Maitland.   Cambridge, 1900.
Hauréau, B. : *Histoire de la philosophie scolastique.*   3 vols.   Paris, 1872.
Henderson, E. F. : *Select Documents of the Middle Ages.*   Bell, 1916.

SOME GREAT MEDIÆVAL THINKERS

JANET, P. : *Histoire de la science politique*, vol. i.   Paris, 1872.

MACKINNON, JAMES : *A History of Modern Liberty*, vol. i.   Longmans, 1906.

POOLE, R. L. : *Illustrations of Medieval Thought and Learning*.   S.P.C.K., 1920.

SCARTAZZINI : *A Companion to Dante*.   Translated from the German by A. J. Butler.   Macmillan, 1893.

SYMONDS, J. A. : *An Introduction to the Study of Dante*.   Black, 1893.

TOYNBEE, P. : *A Concise Dictionary of Proper Names and Notable Matters in the Works of Dante*.   Oxford, 1914.

WICKSTEED, P. : *Dante and Aquinas*.   Dent, 1913.

PIERRE DU BOIS AND THE DOMINATION
OF FRANCE

THERE is perhaps in the whole of mediæval history no century of quite such absorbing interest and charm as the fourteenth. It has suffered from much unmerited detraction at the hands of the mediævalist, who mourns the Golden Age of the twelfth and thirteenth centuries and finds it too modern, and of the modernist, who thinks that all wisdom and beauty dates from what he is pleased to call the Renaissance, and finds it too mediæval. Both have conspired to damn it with the most facile and meaningless of historical epithets as an age of transition. But it is precisely because it is an age of transition that the fourteenth century is of such absorbing interest, for in it much that is finest in the civilisation of the Middle Ages is combined with much that is most characteristic of the modern world. In this century, at one and the same time, the last great struggle of Empire and Papacy marks the culmination and failure of the mediæval experiment in world-organisation, and the young nation-states of Europe first stand out under their rulers, with the mark of their future destiny upon their brows. In this century chivalry makes its last sortie with the Black Prince as its leader and Froissart as its chronicler, and at the same time bourgeois merchants lead chivalry by the nose, and a series of democratic revolts of serfs and artisans prefigure a future more distant yet. There is very little that is attractive in the Middle Ages, and very little that is interesting in our life to-day, that cannot be found in the fourteenth century, if it be sought there.

This combination of mediæval and modern is nowhere more interesting and more characteristic than in the realm of political thought. It is by no means fortuitous that in a series of seven lectures on great mediæval thinkers no less than four should be concerned with writers of the fourteenth century. The fourteenth century insists upon it; and a period which begins with Dante and ends with Wycliffe cannot be lightly dismissed. It may indeed be said that in the history of political thought there are very few periods of equal length to match in importance the first thirty years of this century. During these years wrote Dante, the most gifted exponent of a dream of Empire which had haunted generations of men before him, and Boniface VIII and Agostino Trionfo, the most extreme upholders of papal domination. In these thirty years wrote the splendid trio Marsilio of Padua, John of Jandun, and William of Ockham, who defended the Empire by the evolution of political theories which underlie much of our modern political thought—an Italian, a Frenchman, and an Englishman defending a German prince in an age when scholarship was truly international. And in these thirty years also wrote Pierre Du Bois, mediæval in that the idea of world-dominion still possessed him, but more modern than all the rest, in that he turned contemptuously away from the old problem of the relations of Empire and Papacy, and drew clearly for posterity the lineaments of a national king. The most daring and original of them all, he is so modern that he seems to be writing for a Louis XIV or a Napoleon, rather than for a Philippe le Bel, and yet he is so much a man of his own day that his new ideas struggle out like a butterfly, still half enmeshed in its mediæval chrysalis.

Pierre Du Bois was a Norman, born somewhere about 1255. He studied at the University of Paris, then well advanced upon its famous career. By profession a lawyer, he came into the service of the king of France, and in 1300 we find him at Coutances, exercising the functions of an *avocat royal*, with the special duty of guarding against the encroachments of the ecclesiastical courts upon royal justice. He seems to have amassed a large fortune in pleading causes arising out of clerical property, and his reputation was so high that he was employed by the king of England for a short time in Guienne. But the real interests of Pierre Du Bois were wider than the legal work which occupied his time. He was passionately interested in politics, had (as his latest editor puts it) " the journalist's temperament," and between the years 1300 and 1314 every political crisis found him with a pamphlet, urging some bold scheme upon the Government, or drawing up some line of defence for the King. It is true that he seems to have exercised little influence upon those in authority, and it is posterity, rather than his contemporaries, which has recognised the vigour and originality of his ideas. All his most important works have come down to us anonymously, and only the survival of one piece with his name attached has enabled modern scholars to identify the writer of the others with the *avocat royal*. His theories can be understood only by understanding the peculiar circumstances in which his mind was formed, and which drove him thus to devote his energies to political controversy. It may be said that two facts above all decided the mould into which this original genius was to flow, the first the fact that he was a Frenchman, and the second the fact that he was a lawyer ; for to be a Frenchman, and above all to be a French lawyer, at the beginning of the fourteenth century was of the greatest significance.

Consider first the position of France. She was, had been ever since the twelfth century, a rising power, just at the moment when the Empire, shattered by its fatal struggle with the Papacy, was a falling power. Her greatness was foreshadowed in the eleventh century, when she played such a leading part in the Crusades as to win for them the name of *Gesta Dei per Francos*, and to cause the infidel to give to all Christians the generic name of Franks. It advanced in the twelfth century, when a great renaissance of culture gave France in monasticism, in scholasticism, in literature, in architecture, and in civilisation generally, the leadership of the western world. Her greatness advanced above all with the advance of the French monarchy, which pursued its work of combating the disruptive forces of feudalism and, building on the support of the Church and of the people, approached steadily nearer to its ideal of administrative centralisation on the one hand, while on the other it pushed its frontiers eastward toward the Rhine and southward toward the Alps, wherever opportunity offered. The real pre-eminence of France in Europe was manifest in the middle of the thirteenth century in the career of Louis IX, who embodied and enriched by his personality her claim to leadership. His international position was shown by his leadership of the crusading movement, and by the arbitration which Louis, and not the Emperor, was called upon to give in the disputes of foreign monarchs. Everywhere French was the language of civilisation, while the University of Paris, where the bold Averroist Siger of Brabant and the great orthodox doctor Thomas Aquinas were both teaching, was already in possession of an

intellectual pre-eminence which was to make it in the fourteenth century the only really international power in Europe
and the arbiter of Popes and kings. " France, mère des
armes, des arts, et des lois," had already assumed that *rôle*
in culture which a modern writer has expressed in the
phrase, " Every man has two fatherlands, his own and
France." Moreover, this eminence was without a rival.
The fall of the Hohenstaufen had been a death-blow to
the Empire as a world-power ; and in the struggle the Pope
had come to look upon the king of France, " the eldest
son of the Church," as a counterpoise to the Emperor
and the most powerful of his own supporters. In the
second half of the century there were three French Popes.
In spite of the antiquarian claims of the Emperor, no one
with any sense of reality could doubt that France was the
foremost power in Europe.

In this France Pierre Du Bois was born and the fact
does much to explain the line taken by his political thought.
More significant still was the other fact that he was a
lawyer in the service of the Crown, and to be a lawyer in
the service of the Crown under Philippe le Bel was to be
born to a definite series of ideas. As a counterbalance to
the turbulent nobility of birth and sword, the French
kings raised up this new nobility of the intellect, which
owed everything to its own intelligence and to the royal
favour. Gradually it came to possess the most important
offices of local and central government, and its members
were known as the *chevaliers du roi*. Such was Pierre
Flote, the first layman to become Chancellor of France,
" the little one-eyed *avocat*," as Boniface VIII called him,
who worked all his life for the greatness of the king of
France and died sword in hand at Courtrai. Such was
Guillaume de Nogaret, who dared on behalf of his king

to attack and seize the sacred person of the Pope. And such was Pierre Du Bois himself, one of the boldest speculators of the Middle Ages. "They are not noble," wrote Nogaret of his class, "yet they are knights, *chevaliers du roi*, because the king has taken them to be his men. Thence they draw their honour, their dignity, and they are called the *chevaliers du roi*. They are an infinite number in the realm of France." The characteristics of this band of lawyers were clearly marked; they have been defined as "the knowledge of law, the passion for the royal power, the sentiment of patriotism." Many of the ideas which have sometimes been held to be the original production of Pierre Du Bois were their common possession. "They are the true creators of the modern State by the extension of royal rights," says Funck Brentano, and he quotes the judgment of Renan: "The legists founded that nobility of the robe, of which the first act was to establish the supremacy of the royal power and to diminish the ecclesiastical power, and of which the last act was the Revolution." [1] The political ideas of Pierre Du Bois spring inevitably from these two conditions, that he lived a Frenchman in France, just at the moment when she became the first power in Europe, and that he was one of the *chevaliers du roi*, the band of legists, who were engaged in making the king the first power in France.

What drew forth and formed the theories of Pierre Du Bois was the fact that in his day both these principles were challenged by the Church. France in her turn inherited the struggle which had broken the Empire, though she inherited it in a slightly different form. The octogenarian Pope Boniface VIII, seeing the Emperor as

---

[1] On the *chevaliers du roi* see Funck Brentano, *Le Moyen Âge* (1922), pp. 339–344, and Renan, *Études sur la politique religieuse du règne de Philippe le Bel*, passim.

a conquered foe and the king of France as a subservient
son (for had not the King's brother, Charles of Valois,
invaded Italy to overthrow his enemies in Florence and in
Sicily ?), made for the Papacy the highest claims which
were ever put forward for it, higher than the claims of
Hildebrand, higher even than the claims of Innocent III.
He envisaged himself as head of a vast confederation of
the states of Europe, wielding the temporal as well as the
spiritual power, and asserted his claims in the famous
bulls *Clericis Laicos*, which forbade the clergy to pay taxes
to their lay rulers, and *Unam Sanctam*, which contained the
declaration " that it is necessary to salvation that every
creature should be subject to the Roman Pope." The
climax came in the great Jubilee of 1300, where the legend
of his proud boast, " I am Cæsar, I am Emperor,"
though historically unfounded, is a true expression of his
attitude.

But Boniface was met by the unexpected opposition
of a force new in mediæval politics, the force of national
monarchies. The opposition of the English king, Edward I,
to *Clericis Laicos* and the effective means by which he
expressed it are well known. More epoch-making still
was the opposition of the king of France. A quarrel
broke out which grew more and more bitter ; insults
flew between the eldest son and the Holy Father, and the
affair culminated in the famous outrage of Anagni, when
Guillaume de Nogaret, not without the knowledge of
Philippe le Bel, laid siege to the aged Pope and took him
prisoner. " The tragedy of Anagni must be set against
the tragedy of Canossa." Boniface was unable to survive
the disgrace. He died in indescribable bitterness of
spirit, but his successor, Benedict XI, was powerless to
avenge him, and on his own death shortly afterward a

Frenchman, Bertrand de Got, Archbishop of Bordeaux, was elected Pope in 1305 and never set foot in Italy. The claim of the lay power had been vindicated not by the Empire, but by one of the new nation-states. The Avignon exile had begun and France had simply pocketed the Papacy. She had thus established her own claim to pre-eminence in Europe, but in doing so she had also established the second principle which the Church had threatened, the principle of administrative centralisation and of the king's pre-eminence in his own realm. The stand against *Clericis Laicos*, which would have established the clergy as an *imperium in imperio*, the struggle of the legists, in which Pierre Du Bois was all his life engaged, to defend royal justice against the claims of the ecclesiastical courts, the famous affair of the Templars, in which the King forced the dissolution of that order upon Clement, and the papal palace at Avignon, all were so many assertions that the king was master in his own house.

All through the struggle Pierre Du Bois was pouring out pamphlets, and as a result of the circumstances in which he wrote (for, speculator as he was, there was not one of his works which was not written to meet a particular crisis), his work is dominated by two profound convictions. The first is a conviction of the necessity for French domination in Europe and for the domination of the king in France ; the second is a conviction of the necessity for the utter destruction of the temporal power of the Church, which throughout his life he saw challenging both French domination and royal centralisation. His two most important books are both ostensibly concerned with the best method of obtaining a world-peace (the subject upon which Dante also was during these years exercising his mind and pen), but his real concerns are obviously those described. The earliest work of Pierre Du Bois which has survived is the *Summaria brevis et compendiosa Doctrina felicis Expeditionis et Abbreviationis Guerrarum ac Litium Regni Francorum*, usually known as *De Abbreviatione*.[1] It was written about 1300 and already contains the pith and marrow of his scheme for the aggrandisement of the king of France, the first part containing a plan for world-domination and the second an attack on the ecclesiastical jurisdiction in France. The book upon which his fame rests is, however, the *De Recuperatione Terre Sancte*,[2] written between 1305 and 1307.

The ostensible purpose of the *De Recuperatione Terre Sancte* is to set forth a scheme for a crusade to recover the Holy Land. It cannot be denied that the crusade was something in the nature of an excuse, and that the author was far more interested in the series of political schemes which he had already adumbrated in the *De Abbreviatione*, but it would be a mistake to regard it as a mere excuse, disingenuously put forward by Pierre Du Bois to conceal his real motive. The idea of a crusade was very much in the air at this time, partly because the opening up of intercourse with the Tartars in the Near and Far East had filled the Christian world with the dream of converting them and using their vast power to crush Islam. At any rate, a number of writers of repute produced projects for a crusade during the first decade of the fourteenth century, and it is significant that all were addressed either to the Pope, or to the king of France, or to both. The famous Spanish scholastic, Raymond Lull, sent detailed

---

[1] Analysed by De Wailly in *Bibliothèque de l'École des Chartes*, 1846 (2nd series, iii, 273–315), and more briefly in Renan, *op. cit.*, pp. 290–306. Langlois gives many passages from the original in the notes to his edition of the *De Recuperatione*.

[2] Edited by Ch. V. Langlois in 1891 ; analysed in Renan, *op. cit.*, pp. 317–358.

schemes to the Pope in 1305 and again in 1309;[1] Jacques de Molay, the last Grand Master of the Templars, submitted a plan in 1306, and in the same year Marino Sanuto produced the first draft of his well-known *Liber Secretorum Fidelium Crucis*, which was finally completed and presented to Pope John XXII, together with a map of the world, a chart of the Mediterranean, and plans of Egypt and the Holy Land, in 1321, a copy being sent to the king of France, who was intended to lead the expedition.[2] Guillaume de Nogaret presented Philippe le Bel with a memoir concerning the possibility of a crusade in 1310, and under the influence of Raymond Lull the Council of Vienne took up the idea in 1312. These projects, indeed, continued throughout the century. Pierre Du Bois was in good company.

In the *De Recuperatione Terre Sancte*, which is his masterpiece, Pierre Du Bois brings together all his ideas. It is divided into two parts, the first containing general considerations, of which one copy was dedicated to Edward I, king of England, and another was to go to the Pope, and the second containing certain particular considerations addressed to the king of France, and displaying more openly than would have been decent in the first part his intention for France to dominate the world. He begins by pointing out that a crusade, the great duty of Christendom, is impossible without a general peace among the Christian nations. But how may such a peace be obtained? Only by uniting the whole world under the rule of the king

---

[1] The *De Fine* (the idea of which had been conceived in a letter to the Pope as early as 1288), and the *Liber de Acquisitione Terræ Sanctæ*.

[2] Printed in Bongars, *Gesta Dei per Francos*, ii, 1–288. On Lull and Sanuto see Beazley, *Dawn of Modern Geography*, ii, 310–311, and iii, 309–317, and F. Kunstmann, in *Abhandlungen der histor. Classe der bayer. Akad. der Wissensch.*, vii (1855), 695–819. On crusading projects in general at this time see Renan, *op. cit.*, pp. 354–358.

of France, whose sway, either as direct ruler or as suzerain, must extend over East and West, Moslem and Christian alike ; and the chief means by which this end is to be brought about is by abolishing the temporal power of the Papacy, the cause of so much evil in the past, and transferring it wholesale to the king of France. The funds necessary for the crusade are to be obtained by taking possession of all the lands and temporalities of the regular and secular clergy, paying them in return annual pensions sufficient for their maintenance. He proceeds to detail a scheme for the method to be pursued in the conquest of the Holy Land, which gives him the opportunity to insert a brilliant and original scheme of education. He also draws a careful portrait of an ideal king of France, setting forth his conception of the new monarchy and incidentally his views on legal reform, which are hardly less brilliant and prophetic than his views on education.

It will be seen from this brief synopsis that the book is far-reaching in its scope. How far-reaching is best observed by collecting and illustrating some of Pierre Du Bois' most important ideas from the pages of the *De Recuperatione Terre Sancte* and of the earlier *De Abbreviatione*. Most interesting of all is his twofold dream for France, the dream of world-dominion and of royal centralisation. The sole means by which peace can be obtained is for the world to be subject to the king of France. " It is the peculiar merit of the French to have a surer judgment than other nations, not to act without consideration, nor to place themselves in opposition to right reason." But it is necessary that the king should be born and bred in France and without leaving that happy land should exercise his beneficent rule, for in France the climate is more salubrious and the very stars take on a better aspect and exercise a happier influence than else-where; let the king of England and such "lesser breeds without the Law" take the actual leadership of the crusade; the king of France must stay at home and address himself to the procreation and education of offspring. The bold and simple expedient by which this dream of a world living at peace in submission to France is to be carried out is set forth in both the *De Abbreviatione* and the *De Recuperatione*. The idea of transferring the temporal power of the Papacy to the French king is the basis of all Pierre Du Bois' speculations. He worked at it, added to it, reproduced it at every crisis, eagerly seizing on such events as seemed to place it nearer attainment and striving to get it brought before the King. There is a certain comedy in his bland assumption that the world could be set upside down with ease, if only the king of France would bestir himself and do it. Country by country he indicates the method to be employed. The Pope exercises full imperial rights over the lands comprised in the Donation of Constantine and over those rulers who have done him homage. Let him give up these temporal rights, together with the title of senator of Rome, to the French king, who will then receive not only the papal patrimony in Italy, but the suzerainty over Naples, Sicily, Aragon, Hungary, and England, which are vassals of the Pope (this part of the scheme was not contained in the copy sent to Edward I). Lombardy, it is true, holds of the Emperor, but there should be no difficulty in obtaining its cession from him or from the Electors by treaty, since the false Lombards are always in revolt and their ruler is well aware of the hopelessness of reducing them; the king of France, of course, would have no difficulty in bringing them to heel. Influence in Spain must be secured by armed intervention on behalf of the Infantas of La Cerda, grandsons of St Louis of France, who have been unjustly despoiled of their rights and should be given the kingdoms of Granada and Portugal to hold as vassals of France.

Germany troubled this bold dreamer. In the *De Abbreviatione* of 1300 he says that the outcome must be trusted to the God of Battles, a not uncommon conclusion among professed peace-lovers of his type; alternatively it is possible that before long the king of Germany will need Philip's help, and then a deal can be done; meanwhile, at any rate, the heirs to the German throne, sons of Philip's sister, who had recently married Rudolph of Austria, can be educated at the French court. In the *De Recuperatione* of 1305–7 he suggests that the alliance of the Habsburgs can be gained by helping them to make the Imperial crown hereditary in their house. In 1308, on the death of Albert I, a better idea strikes him, and he will have Philip of France himself stand as a candidate for the crown of Germany. Throughout it is clear that he regards Germany as a national kingdom like any other, and is untroubled by any conception of the Empire as an international power.

Not content with securing her influence over the West by these schemes, Pierre Du Bois will have France dominant in the East also. In 1300 he suggests that Charles of Valois, Philip's brother, shall marry Catherine de Courtenay, heiress of the Latin empire of Constantinople; and indeed the marriage took place shortly afterward. In the *De Recuperatione* he has plans for a crusade which will not only conquer the Moslem East for Philip, but will enforce Charles of Valois' claim on Constantinople against the usurping Greek emperor; and in 1308 his soaring ambition leads him to write a new pamphlet, urging the creation of an empire there for the King's son, Philippe le Long.[1] Thus East and West, by a process apparently as simple as knocking down ninepins, the dominion of France is to be secured. *Q.E.F.*

It must be admitted that these chimerical schemes do not show our author at his best. More interesting is his portrait of a national king, the conception which the legists were gradually evolving. If his view of peace by world-dominion is mediæval, his view of a national king is essentially modern. His is the first real delineation of the modern state in the history of political ideas. He lays stress on the independence of the royal power of all other authorities ; the Emperor is dependent upon the Pope, because he receives from the Pope his crown ; not so the king of France ; the heir of St Peter has no claim over him ; his power is inherent and knows no superior authority. Pierre Du Bois strikes out (characteristically in a parenthesis) the principle of the necessary obedience of the subject to the powers that be, a doctrine which was destined in the hands of Luther to play so great a part in moulding political thought. When speaking of a possible armed reduction of the Lombards by the king of France, should they rebel after he has received the suzerainty over them from the Emperor, he says that such a reduction would be legitimate, " for nothing could authorise them to refuse obedience to their prince." He sets forth also the conception of the king as guardian of religion in his kingdom, a defender of the faith whose duty it is to watch over true religion, which the Papacy betrays. It was once more an idea which became familiar at the time of the Reformation. His whole ideal is one of administrative unity, of

---

[1] This short and interesting pamphlet is printed by Langlois as an appendix to his edition of the *De Recuperatione*, pp. 131–140.

highly centralised government. It is the ideal which became characteristic of the Renaissance state, and which never ceased to inspire French politicians, whether the ministers of Louis XIV or the Jacobins of 1793. His strongest attack is reserved for the enemy with which he is most familiar, the ecclesiastical courts, which seek to steal more and more cases from the royal justice, and for the temporal possessions of the Church, which form an *imperium in imperio* and prevent the complete control, the rigid centralisation, which must be the royal object. But he has a strong idea of the duties as well as the rights of this national king. All power is in his hands, no local or sectional liberties may stand before him, but he rules because he embodies his people's interests. Pierre Du Bois criticises severely Philippe le Bel's injustices in the levy of taxation, his debasement of the coinage, his unfair exaction of military services. The king is the embodiment of the law, but he is bound by it. Incidentally he sets out some very interesting and original views on the law itself and on the administration of justice. He is of Langland's opinion upon the length and expense of lawsuits : " Lawe is so lordeliche and loth to make ende." They must be shortened and made cheaper. Moreover, the law itself is too complicated and chaotic. It must be reduced to a single code, clearly and logically set out, purged of inconsistencies, able to be consulted with ease. He shows himself here at his most prophetic, for what is this, as Renan has pointed out, but the juridical ideal of the Revolution ? What is this but the Code Napoléon, envisaged five centuries before its appearance by the legist of Philippe le Bel ?

This conception of the position of France in Europe and of the king in France is the real pith of Pierre Du Bois' political system. But other ideas worked out in his books are worthy of notice. One is his attack on the temporal power of the Church. In the course of this he gives a detailed and very interesting indictment of the condition of the Church in his own day, attacking in turn Pope, cardinals, secular clergy, and religious orders, and showing that the true reason of their misdeeds and of their failure to perform their religious duties lies in their possession of property and exercise of temporal rule.[1] The Pope's attempts to enforce his temporal jurisdiction only hinder his spiritual power. "Wars therefore are stirred up, numbers of princes are condemned by the Church, together with their adherents, and thus die more men than can be counted, whose souls probably go down to hell and whom nevertheless it is the Pope's duty to save. . . . Because of his sanctity the Pope should aspire only to the glory of pardoning, praying, giving judgment in the name of the Church, preserving peace among Catholic princes, so as to bring souls safe to God ; but he shows himself to be the author, promoter, and exerciser of many wars and homicides, and sets an evil example. It depends on him to conserve his ordinary resources without being turned from the care of souls ; it is in his hands to rid himself of worldly occasions and to avoid the cause of so many evils. If he will not accept so great an advantage, will he not incur the reproaches of all men for his cupidity, pride, and bold presumption ? " Let the Pope therefore hand over his temporal authority to the French king, receiving in exchange an adequate annual pension, and let him continue to exercise his spiritual authority. In the *De Recuperatione*, the election of Clement V having already brought about a situation somewhat similar to that

[1] Incidentally he disapproves of the celibacy of the clergy.

envisaged by Pierre Du Bois, our author draws an idyllic picture of Clement, all wars ended, the traps of the perfidious Romans and Lombards escaped, and his temporal goods abandoned, living happy days in his native land of France. Since Roman Popes have abused the papal power, Rome must lose for ever the honour of possessing the Papacy, and the Pope must remain in France and create French cardinals, until the Papacy becomes to all intents and purposes a French bishopric. He anticipates here the long Avignon exile and the later history of the Gallican Church, always jealous of ultramontane control.

Turning to the secular Church as a whole, he urges that the goods of the bishops should be handed over to laymen, who will in return furnish them with an adequate pension. He is equally hostile to the regular Church, especially to the Benedictines, though he evidently has a kindness for the friars. The goods of the monasteries are to be given in trust to laymen, who will pay out the annual incomes. His views on nunneries are interesting; the number of nuns in each is to be drastically reduced and wherever possible they are to be converted into schools for girls. The military orders are to be suppressed and their goods used for the conquest of the Holy Land; that this was not a mere dream the suppression of the Templars shortly afterward shows. It is obvious that this attack on the temporalities of the Church fitted in very well with Pierre Du Bois' conception of the royal power. It would have placed in the king's hands enormously valuable resources, which might or might not be used for educational purposes, or for the purposes of a crusade. Again the Reformation faces us in his schemes, and the lineaments of his national king are the familiar lineaments of Henry VIII, *Defensor Fidei*, spoiler of the monasteries, " the mighty lord who broke the bonds of Rome."

Perhaps, however, the most original section of Pierre Du Bois' great treatise, as it is certainly the most enthralling, is that which gives us his views upon education. It comes in as a pendant to his ideas on the best method of carrying on the crusade. The Nestorian Christians of the East must be united to the Catholic Church ; the conquered Moslems must be converted ; but how is this to be done, when the Christians possess so few and such inferior inter-preters ? It is necessary to send to them men skilled in their languages, able to argue with them ; never was the gift of tongues more sorely needed. The Pope, therefore, must create a new band of interpreters, learned in all the languages of the East, a sort of Civil Service to follow in the wake of armies and to accompany ambassadors. He must order the foundation of schools for boys and girls in the priories of the Templars and Hospitallers in each province, with a central school for the most advanced scholars at Rome itself. The children are to be chosen at the age of four, five, or six years, and are never to return to their parents, unless the latter are willing to repay the cost of their education. They are first to be taught Latin and then some are to specialise in Greek, some in Arabic, some in each of the languages of the East. They are not only to learn Oriental languages ; some are to make a special study of surgery and medicine, some of the veterinary art, some of civil and canon law, some of astronomy, some of mathe-matical and natural science, and some of theology. Nor are physical exercises and the mechanical arts to be omitted.[1] The girls are to be brought up like the boys to learn Latin and also grammar, logic, and one Oriental language. They

[1] For his detailed description see *De Recup.*, pp. 49–53, 58–70.

are then to go on to the study of surgery and medicine. Above all, they must be so well instructed in the Christian doctrine that they will be able to teach it to unbelievers. It must be confessed that a certain feminist enthusiasm, awakened by reading the schemes of Pierre Du Bois for women's education, is rather dashed by the discovery that the destiny of these learned blue stockings is to be given in marriage to Oriental prelates and rulers, in order that they may convert their husbands. Stubbs was wont to say that everything was in the *De Recuperatione*, including the new woman;[1] one feels inclined to revise his dictum and to declare that everything is in it, including the old Adam. Pierre Du Bois declares that the women will aid greatly by their knowledge of Church doctrine and also of medicine and surgery, an acute prevision of modern missionary tactics. He considers that the women of the East will lend themselves to marriages between these learned ladies and the Saracen chiefs for the sake of the advantages of monogamy, which the spread of Christianity will introduce; though how monogamy would benefit them, seeing that the available supply of husbands was simultaneously to be lessened by the importation of Christian wives, he does not pause to explain.

Another striking anticipation of modern political thought is to be found in Pierre Du Bois' scheme for securing international peace among Christian rulers, as the necessary prelude to a crusade. A general council of princes and prelates is to be called by the Pope; here it is to be ordained that full justice shall be done to all who complain of any wrong, according to the laws and customs of the different kingdoms, by the judges appointed for this purpose. No Catholic is to take arms against a Catholic, and those who

[1] Figgis, *From Gerson to Grotius*, p. 27.

wish to fight shall fight against the infidel. Pierre Du Bois suggests suitable punishments for those who, despite this ordinance, rush into war with their brethren, and here he anticipates the weapon for reducing recalcitrant states known in our own day as the economic boycott. " If any shall presume, contrary to this good ordinance, to make war against their Catholic brothers they shall forthwith incur the loss of all their goods, and so also shall all those who aid them by fighting, victuals, arms, or other necessities of life or of warfare, of any description ; and after the end of the war the survivors, of whatever age, condition, and sex, shall be for ever removed from their possessions, and they and their heirs shall be sent to populate the Holy Land. . . . Thus therefore those who begin a war, and those who wilfully lend them help and counsel, communicate with them, or supply them with any manner of victuals, water, fire, or other necessities of life, shall be punished by the lord Pope, and they shall not be excommunicated nor anathematised, in order to avoid the danger to their souls and an increase in the numbers of the damned ; for it is far better to punish them temporally than eternally."

Pierre Du Bois recognises, however, the need for some method of settling disputes, which cannot be dealt with by existing courts of law. " But since these cities [the Italian republics] and many princes, recognising no superiors in their lands, who may do them justice according to the laws and customs of the localities, will strive to enter into disputes, before whom are they to proceed and to take litigation ? It may be replied that the [general] council must ordain the election of three religious or lay arbitrators, prudent, experienced, and faithful men, who shall be sworn to choose three prelates as judges, and three other persons from each side, men of substance, and such as are obviously incapable of being corrupted by love, hate, fear, greed, or anything else. These shall come together in a suitable place, and having been strictly sworn, and presented before their coming with the articles of the petition and the defence, fully set forth, shall receive witnesses and instruments, and, first rejecting all that is superfluous and beside the point, shall diligently examine them. They shall listen to the examination of each witness by at least two men, sworn and faithful and true; the depositions shall be written down and very diligently examined, and most carefully kept by the judges, to prevent fraud and falsehood. . . . In giving judgment, if it be expedient, let them have assessors who are to their knowledge faithful and skilled in divine and canon and civil law. If either party be discontented with their sentence the same judges shall send the process and judgment to the apostolic seat, for it to be amended or altered by the Supreme Pontiff for the time being, as shall seem good to him, or if not, to be confirmed for a perpetual memorial and registered in the chronicles of the Holy Roman Church." Those who are familiar with the constitution of the League of Nations will agree that this is a remarkable forecast to have been produced by a fourteenth-century writer.[1]

It remains to attempt some estimate of the value of Pierre Du Bois as a political thinker. Here it is necessary to guard against exaggeration. He is not completely original, for no man can be other than the product of his age, and a great deal that he set forth was already in the air. His conception of a national king was founded upon the actual facts of the French king's power and the beginnings of a conscious sense of nationality both in England and in France, where they were manifested in the resistance of

---

[1] See *De Recup.*, §§ 3, 4, 12.

both rulers and peoples to the demands of the Popes. Pierre Du Bois only sets out coherently the ideal at which all the *chevaliers du roi* were aiming. Moreover, even his wild dreams of world-dominion for the French king were not unshared by other mediæval thinkers. John of Jandun in one of his treatises observes, " The monarchical rule of the universe belongs to the very illustrious and sovereign kings of France ";[1] and in 1329 a French missionary in India, Jordan Catala by name, wrote to Avignon : " I believe that the king of France could subject the whole world to himself and to the Christian faith without anyone else to aid him." [2]

The attack on the temporalities of the Church was not new either. Arnold of Brescia, the Waldenses, and other heretical sects of the twelfth century had made it before Pierre Du Bois. So had that other modern, the Emperor Frederick II, so apt at irritating Popes ; in a manifesto addressed to all Christian princes he declared : " God is our witness that our intention has always been to force churchmen to follow in the footsteps of the primitive Church, to live an apostolic life and to be humble like Jesus Christ. In our days the Church has become worldly. We therefore propose to do a work of charity in taking away from such men the treasures with which they are filled for their eternal damnation " (1245).[3] The nobles of France even formed a society for the disendowment of the Church, rather in the light of a good investment than of a disinterested desire for ecclesiastical reform. In Pierre Du Bois' own day the same ideas were being most strenuously preached by the left wing of the Franciscan order. Indeed he wrote on the eve of that struggle between the Emperor

---

[1] Lavisse, *Hist. de France*, iii (by Ch. V. Langlois), 290.
[2] *Medieval France*, ed. Tilley (1922), p. 102.
[3] Quoted in Tout, *Empire and Papacy, 918–1273*, p. 389.

Lewis the Bavarian and the Pope John XXII, of which one
of the main issues was to be the condemnation of ecclesiastical property by the Fraticelli.

The question of the importance of the study of foreign
languages was also much discussed at the time. Three
Popes had already concerned themselves with it, and as
early as 1248 Innocent IV had directed a bull to the
Chancellor of the University of Paris announcing that he
had sent certain boys, skilled in Arabic and other Oriental
languages, to Paris, in order that they might study theology
and afterward go out as missionaries to the heathen.
The advocacy of the study of science and of Oriental languages was part of a general movement to widen the bases
of knowledge, as well as to convert the infidel, in which
the University of Paris took the lead. It was one of the
dearest projects of Raymond Lull, and the Council of
Vienne actually established chairs in Greek and Oriental
Languages at Paris in 1312.[1]

Moreover, if he was not entirely original even in his
' modern ' views, it must also be admitted that Pierre Du
Bois' mind could never entirely shake off mediæval con-
ventions. His thought runs in the old mould of world-
empire, though from it he shapes something new. He
oscillates between the most radical attack on papal power
and a trust in papal authority to obtain some of his desires,
such as the imperial crown for his master, and between
a condemnation of the misuse of excommunication and a
tendency to fall back upon it to provide the ultimate
sanction for some of his schemes. He has also a very
imperfect sense of what can and what cannot be accomplished in actual fact, which probably accounts for his lack

[1] See note by Langlois in his edition of *De Recup.*, p. 47, and *Medieval France*, ed. Tilley, p. 234.

of influence at court. His plan of world-dominion ignores the fact that the king of England may not agree to do homage to France, and that the Lombard cities may prove as hard to conquer as the Flemish cities were proving even as he wrote. He is the most curious mixture of *Realpolitik* and of the wildest chimeras. Similarly, in his schemes for the conquest of the East his educational system, in itself so remarkable, is based on two large and most unlikely assumptions, the first that well-bred and well-educated European ladies will be willing to intermarry on a large scale with Orientals, and the second (as Renan points out) that Orientals have only to be familiar with our civilisation to perceive at once its essential superiority to their own, though it must be admitted that there is nothing specially mediæval about this attitude of mind, which has enjoyed a persistence worthy of a better psychology.

What is original and modern and striking about Pierre Du Bois, what makes his book one of the most remarkable treatises of the Middle Ages (the more attractive because it is so admirably concise and short), is the temper of his mind, his essentially philosophic outlook, his scorn of the literal use of Biblical texts to make debating points, and of the absurd ramifications of the sun and moon argument, above all his openness to new ideas and his dislike (truly remarkable in a lawyer) of an unintelligent conservatism, whose only criterion is precedent. This temper is nowhere better expressed than in the well-known passage in the *De Recuperatione* in which he pleads that new situations should be met by new measures. " Does not Averroës say that the Arabs suffered many evils, because they believed that their laws were to be universally maintained and never modified ? Was not all civil and statute law made in order to be right and fitting ? For there can hardly be found anything in the world which should be right and fitting in all places, at all seasons, and for all persons. Therefore the laws and statutes of men vary with the varying places, seasons, and persons ; and many philosophers have taught that this should be so, because expediency clearly demands it, and the Lord and Master of all sciences, of the holy Fathers, and of the philosophers, in order that He might teach us to do so without fear, changed many things in the New Testament, which He had ordained in the Old." [1]

When all is said and done there can be few books more remarkable in their prevision of the future than the *De Recuperatione*. If Dante's *De Monarchia* was " an epitaph rather than a prophecy," Pierre Du Bois' book was a prophecy rather than a programme. What is his project of world-peace but Sully's " Grand Design " and Emeric Crucé's " New Cyneas "? [2] What is his conception of a national king ruling over a centralised realm but the conception of Machiavelli and Luther, the conception of the Renaissance ? His picture of the French monarch dazzling all the world would not have seemed exaggerated to the sixteenth century, when Maximilian, king of the Romans, was wont " playfully to say more than once that if he were God and had several children he would make the eldest God after him, but the second he would make him king of France "; [3] it would not have seemed exaggerated

---

[1] *De Recup.*, § 48, p. 39.

[2] It is more like the " Grand Design " than the " New Cyneas," since the former likewise was only a means for the world-dominion of the king of France ; but it anticipates the latter in its insistence upon economic pressure and a court of international arbitration. It may also be compared with Cardinal Alberoni's project, which had the same ostensible object of a crusade against the Turks. See Jacob ter Meulen, *Der Gedanke der Internationalen Organisation in seiner Entwicklung, 1300–1800* (Haag, 1917), *passim*.

[3] Quoted from Claude de Seissel, *Hist. singulière du Roy Loys XII* (Paris, 1558), p. 69, by Jusserand in *American Hist. Review*, xxvii (1922), 447.

to the seventeenth century, when half Europe was in arms
to prevent it from coming true politically, as it was true
culturally, in the rule of Louis XIV ; it would not have
seemed exaggerated to the early nineteenth century, when
all minds were fixed on the life-and-death struggle with
Napoleon. It is true that the idea of world-empire was
mediæval, but Pierre Du Bois wears his mediævalism with
a difference. His world-empire has a national and territorial basis ; it is something new, at once more Roman
and less Holy than the mediæval Empire. That twofold
dream of French domination in Europe and of royal
domination in France (world-empire without, complete
administrative centralisation within) is the ideal for which
Richelieu struggled, which Louis XIV for a time achieved,
which the French Revolution revived, and which found
its apotheosis in Napoleon. Not only did Napoleon
realise in France and in Europe what seemed the wildest
dreams of Pierre Du Bois, but his attitude toward the
Papacy was exactly the same. " For the Pope I am Charlemagne, since like Charlemagne I unite the crown of France
with that of the Lombards, while my empire stretches over
the East." Pierre Du Bois also quoted Charlemagne.

Again, how modern is his conception of French domination in the East and how steadily France has pursued
it throughout modern times ; Francis I's alliance with
Suleiman the Magnificent, and the Capitulations which
made France the first power in the Near East in the sixteenth century ; the commercial supremacy of France in
the Levant in the seventeenth century ; Napoleon's dream
of an Eastern empire stretching over Syria and Egypt—
perhaps to India itself ; the part played by France in the
Eastern Question throughout the nineteenth century ;
the emergence of a French colonial and Moslem empire

in Northern Africa in the twentieth century; the Angora treaty and the French *entente* with the Kemalists, which so perturbed English politicians of late; they are all pre-figured by Pierre Du Bois. Indeed, one is tempted still further to extend Stubbs' epigram and to say that not only the new woman, but also M. Franklin Bouillon, is to be found in his book. This man, before they came to birth, delineated the Renaissance monarch and the Gallican Church, laid down the legal ideal formulated in the Code Napoléon, foreshadowed the policy of modern France in the East, set out a scheme for the peaceful settlement of international disputes by means of an international court of arbitration, and struck off in passing the higher educa-tion of women, the School of Oriental Studies, the medical missionary, and the economic boycott. However wild may be some of his practical proposals, however much he owes to his contemporaries, and however he may still be clogged by the conceptions of the Middle Ages, Pierre Du Bois was an original thinker and a herald of the modern world.

EILEEN POWER

BIBLIOGRAPHY

A. PRIMARY SOURCES

Works of Pierre Du Bois

The *De Abbreviatione* is analysed by Wailly in " Bibliothèque de l'École des Chartes," 2me série, iii (1846).

Several short treatises are printed in Dupuy, *Hist. du différend d'entre le Pape Boniface VIII et Philippe le Bel; Preuves* (1655).

The *De Recuperatione Terre Sancte* is edited by Ch. V. Langlois (in the " Coll. des Textes pour servir à l'Étude de l'Histoire"; Paris, 1891).

A list of Pierre Du Bois' works will be found at the end of Professor Powicke's paper mentioned below.

SOME GREAT MEDIÆVAL THINKERS

B. Secondary Sources

Renan, *Études sur la politique religieuse du règne de Philippe le Bel* (1899), contains a brilliant study of Pierre Du Bois and an analysis of his writings.

F. M. Powicke: "Pierre Du Bois, a Medieval Radical," in *Historical Essays by Members of Owens College, Manchester*, ed. T. F. Tout and J. Tait (1902).

Ch. V. Langlois: Introduction to his edition of the *De Recuperatione*, and in Lavisse, *Hist. de France*, iii (1901), 284–291.

J. N. Figgis: "A Forgotten Radical," in the *Cambridge Review*, 1899.

On the period in general see Boutaric, *La France sous Philippe le Bel* (1901), and Ch. V. Langlois, in Lavisse, *Hist. de France*, iii, Part II (1901).

VII

MARSILIO OF PADUA AND MEDIÆVAL SECULARISM

THE far-famed and remarkable book called *Defensor Pacis* was completed and presented to the Emperor Ludwig of Bavaria (Louis IV) in the year 1324. It will be well to consider, first, some few of the things that this date means. Just about twenty years earlier, the conflict between the Pope and the Government of France had reached a crisis. In the year 1298, in a bull known as *Sacrosanctæ Ecclesiæ*, Boniface VIII had claimed for the Pope a *plenitudo potestatis* over all persons and causes in Christendom and, using a phrase from Roman law-books, had asserted that all law was in the Pope's heart. It was an assertion of sovereignty absolute and unlimited, save by that law divine of which the Pope himself was the interpreter. In 1302, in the bull *Unam Sanctam*, the Pope had further expounded and defended his claim. But, in that same year, Philip IV's Government had succeeded in securing support from all classes in France for its utter repudiation of the Pope's doctrine and its utter defiance of his threats. In 1303 the University of Paris had associated itself with its King's attitude and with his appeal from the Pope to a General Council. Then, on September 27, 1303, had occurred the terrible scene at Anagni. In 1305, two years after the tragic death of Pope Boniface, the French monarchy had completed its triumph by securing the election of a French Pope, the consequent establishment of a French majority in the College of Cardinals, and, subsequently, the transference of the seat of the Papacy from Rome to Avignon. Yet even then the Pope had not drained to the bottom the cup of his humiliation. He drank it to the dregs in the years that followed. In 1310 there began before the new French Pope at Avignon the trial of the dead Pope Boniface, on charges formulated by the French Government. To escape from finding, before all Christendom, that Pope Boniface VIII had been a monster of iniquity, his successor had to sacrifice the Templars.

It was an amazing series of events, of which, I think, the full significance has hardly yet been brought out. The action of the French Government had been such as might well, only a hundred years earlier, have produced a crusade against France. Yet, practically, no one had lifted a finger on the Pope's behalf. His exposition of the dream of a theocratic Christendom under the sole sovereignty of a Pope with two swords had aroused no kind of responsive movement. Christendom was hostile or ·contemptuous or indifferent. The bubble so assiduously blown for the last two centuries had reached its limit of expansion and suddenly burst. The humiliation was profound; the loss of prestige enormous. To say that the Papacy never recovered from this blow is, in a sense, true; but it was not the action or the mere immediate triumph of Philip IV that was decisive. What made recovery impossible was the prevalence of the points of view that action had expressed or implied.

Pope Boniface VIII had challenged all secular governments. Developing to its extreme logical conclusions a theory implied in Hildebrand's letters more than two hundred years earlier, he had asserted, in the face of the

168

growing national monarchies in France and in England, that absolute sovereignty belonged to the Pope, that all secular law derived validity only from his sanction, that there was but one real authority in Christendom. Because the end and purpose of life is the same for all men and transcends this world of sense, because all men are one in Christ and the Pope is the Vicar of Christ and the voice of the Church Universal, therefore in the Pope must reside an authority that cannot be limited by custom or device of man. To say that there exists any authority independent of the Pope is blasphemy. To that challenge the reply of the French Government had been immediate and, in a sense, crushing. But that reply had been an appeal to force rather than an appeal to reason. The French monarchy had not clearly stated its case : it had preferred to make its appeal to fears and hatreds, jealousies and cupidities. It had not stated the real issue. It had implied much and defined nothing. On the sensational events of the struggle Pierre Du Bois had indeed supplied a sort of running commentary. But the constructive effort, the effort to formulate a theory alternative to that of the papal bulls, came after the event.

The first great literary and philosophic comment on what had happened, the first great attempt at a new construction, was Dante's *De Monarchia*, written between 1310 and 1313. But Dante altogether mistook the issue. That was no longer, if ever it really had been, an issue between Pope and Emperor. The issue was between theocratic sovereignty based on recognition of a transcendental purpose in life and secular sovereignties based on recognition of earthly and localised needs. The Papacy, as temporal power, was mortally wounded already ; but the Empire was already dead. The real fact, I think, is that the mediæval Empire had been still-born. Both Du Bois and John of Paris had pointed out its obsoleteness. Dante's book was a fine piece of imaginative construction ; but it was off the point. It was not, really, what it has been said to be, the swan-song of something dying : it was, rather, an attempt to resuscitate the dead. And then, some ten years after the *De Monarchia*, came the *Defensor Pacis*.

No one during the fourteenth century seems to have doubted that the *Defensor Pacis* was the joint work of two men, Marsilio of Padua and John of Jandun. For a long time past, however, it has been very generally, though not universally, declared that John of Jandun had very little or even nothing at all to do with it. Very good grounds exist, in my opinion, for believing that this view is entirely wrong. It is not necessary to discuss here this question of authorship : but there are a few things worth saying about the reputed authors.

Padua, it may be remembered, not quite irrelevantly, was the city of Ezzelino da Romano : one might almost say the city of the Emperor Frederick II. Marsilio was born there about the year 1270, some ten years after Ezzelino came to his end. Hatred and fear of Milan had made Padua Ghibelline and kept it Ghibelline. Marsilio must have grown up in an atmosphere strongly anti-papal and even anti-clerical. He led a wandering and adventurous life. At one time he was a canon of Padua, at another a soldier of fortune. Later he went to Paris. He took there the degree of Master of Arts, and in 1312 he was Rector of the University for the statutory period of three months. He must have been at Paris in the years of the trial of Pope Boniface. He seems to have remained there till 1324, by which time the city had become, apparently, an unsafe place of residence for him. Evidently he was an energetic, restless, and adventurous person ; and that he was animated by virulent hatred not only of the Papacy but of the clergy in general is proved by his writing.

It was, presumably, at Paris that Marsilio met John of Jandun.   He was a member of the university, a canon of Senlis after 1306, and he wrote some philosophical commentaries on Aristotle.   Very little is known about him ; but he seems to have been associated with the party in the university that had supported Siger of Brabant and which was more or less tainted with Averroism.   The combination of a Paduan and of a man in sympathy with Siger was certainly likely to produce something a little startling. When, in 1327, the Pope described these two persons as "pupils of damnation" and their book as " full of heresies," I fancy that, from his own point of view, he was even more right than he thought he was.   I doubt whether they were heretics in the strict sense : I doubt whether either of them was a Christian in any sense at all, in spite of the display of scriptural texts in the *Defensor*.   We all know that the devil himself can quote Scripture.

Language has sometimes been used about the *Defensor* which implies that the book did not really belong to its time and was, in some obscure sense, unmediæval.   Such language seems to me grotesquely false.   The thought of the book has a long history.   It expressed something at least very like what had been the thought of Pierre Flotte and Guillaume de Nogaret : it expressed also that fierce hatred of Pope and clergy which was generated in the furious civic and faction struggles of thirteenth-century Italy.   It had its main root, I think, in the thought and teaching of the law schools of Bologna and Montpellier, in the latter of which both Pierre Flotte and Guillaume de Nogaret had been students.   It expressed, too, something

171

of that philosophic scepticism and that un-Christian or anti-Christian speculation that was rife at Paris before 1300. If one seeks adumbrations of or approximations to its theory one has only to go to Pierre Du Bois and John of Paris. Its appearance in 1324 is in no way whatever surprising : some such book was, I think, bound to appear just about then. It dealt with questions that were being more and more discussed. It was, indeed, almost topical. That it belonged very completely to its own time is shown by the fact that it remained very much alive all through the fourteenth century. Fifty years after its appearance, the Pope was making anxious inquiries at Paris about a French translation that was said to have been issued. If the year 1324 belongs to the Middle Ages the book was certainly thoroughly mediæval.

It has often been said, too, that the *Defensor* was in advance of its time. This phrase always seems to me a foolish one. I can give no meaning to it that does not involve strange assumptions. I own to a dim notion that when someone says that the thought of a book was far ahead of its time he really means that the view it expresses is nearer his own than the views of most people at that time were. But I confess I regard that fact as of no importance or significance whatever.

The *Defensor* is a remarkable book in many ways, and under the circumstances of the moment it was a rather bold book. Not that it was really so very audacious. The audacity of Marsilio is little to that of Siger ; and both he and his colleague may be said actually to have made their fortunes by the book. Indubitably it possesses originality; but as to the extent of its originality I am doubtful. There was nothing really peculiar about its virulent abuse of Pope and clergy or its hatred of papal and clerical claims. As to its philosophy, I am doubtful how far that would have seemed new at either Bologna or Montpellier.

Limits of space absolutely forbid me any attempt to give even a summarily complete account of the content of the *Defensor* : and I may say that, in my view, no adequate account of that content yet exists in print. The book is a difficult one, for many reasons. The difficulty, I incline to believe, arises partly from its being the product of two very different minds, with very different modes of thought. Up to a certain point the two agree : beyond that point their views remain unreconciled. However that may be, the book is undeniably afflicted with grave inconsistencies. The authors set side by side as mere alternatives propositions which are mutually exclusive. There are very many ambiguities ; many things half said, many suggestions that are made and dropped. Frequently the writer seems to be reaching out after an idea that he never quite gets into focus.

Apart from all that, there is another difficulty of a specific kind. All through the more philosophical portion of the book the writer is manifestly struggling with the difficulties of an insufficient terminology. He could not quite find words to express his conceptions ; and he was not, perhaps, quite clear enough, himself, to see where the difficulty lay. Defective terminology was, I think, a serious difficulty for all the later mediæval thinkers. They wrote, and presumably they thought, in Latin ; but it was a Latin that never quite fitted, torture and twist it as they might. It would be absurd to say that it was a foreign language to them ; yet it was not in the full sense their own. To some extent, indeed, the language of mediæval philosophy was a language which the schools had made for themselves. But the more technically they used its terms, the more, in the long run, were they hampered in trying to express thought which had never yet found coherent and logical expression. And this is precisely what, at all events in Part I of the *Defensor*, the authors were trying to do. They were trying to express something more than had been formally expressed before ; and they had to express it in terms which obscured or only partially conveyed their meaning. If it were difficult for them to express their thought accurately, it is, obviously, yet more difficult for us to understand what they meant.

I do not think any scholar really knows mediæval Latin well enough, or can do so. Many of us, in reading mediæval Latin, must surely have been struck by an odd bareness and dryness, a lack of colour, a lack of ring. One feels, at times, that the writer is at once extraordinarily intellectual and extraordinarily dull. It is like listening to a voice that is absolutely toneless or monotonous. It is, of course, true that the language of philosophy tends naturally to be inhumanly toneless. But in mediæval writings we find this quality where we certainly should not expect to find it. I have often been struck by the seeming impossibility of feeling sure whether a particular passage is ironic or simply naïve. Such a doubt could hardly exist if we understood not merely the dictionary meaning of the words used, but the associations they carried. The significance of words is very largely dependent on associations. To fail to catch them is ignorance of the language. It is just this, I think, that in mediæval Latin we constantly miss.

I will give an instance of what I meant when I spoke of defective terminology. It is not an altogether good instance ; but it is in some ways a crucial one. In discussing the bases of human society the authors of the

Defensor habitually use the word *regnum*. What does this word mean? It might, for a moment, be supposed that it referred specifically to the kingdom of France; but what is said of it, as well as the highly abstract nature of the whole discussion, makes that quite impossible. The word cannot even be securely translated ' kingdom,' since in some passages it is clearly implied that the *regnum* need not have a king. But can we translate *regnum* simply by our phrase ' the State '? That, I think, is the best we can do. But there are difficulties : there are questions that must be asked and cannot well be answered. Why do the authors use *regnum* rather than *respublica*? Did they conceive Padua as a *regnum* and Jacopo Carrara as a *rex*? There are passages which might suggest that the *regnum* is the universal monarchy of the Emperor : there are others that indicate that it cannot be so. Did the authors already see Christendom as a system of rightfully independent states? It is not impossible. Such a conception, or something very like it, had been already expressed by John of Paris. But, if so, why do they not say so? All one can say is that they use the word *regnum* to connote something in their minds that answered more nearly to our phrase ' the State ' than to anything else. I will not go farther. There remains an ambiguity.

The most that can be done here is to attempt a summary of what seems most essential in the content of the *Defensor*. The doing of that involves a certain simplification. Difficulties must to some extent be evaded ; ambiguities must be passed over, and inconsistencies that do not seem radical must be ignored. To do all this will be to make the thought of the book clearer than it really is. But at least I will try not to represent the authors as saying anything they do not say.

The starting-point, logically, is the account given by the writers of the origin of political society. Here the main assertion they make seems to be this : that what we call the State originates in a general recognition of common needs. It evolves from the family ; but the family itself involves no such recognition. It existed for no common good, but solely for the good of its head. Then followed an association of families, and this association was brought about by two recognitions. There was, firstly, the recognition that there were certain needs common to all men, and, secondly, the recognition that the powers of man, or of the family, in isolation, were insufficient to his need. At every step of this account Aristotle is quoted or referred to ; but the authors do not altogether agree with Aristotle.

Political society starts, then, with a realisation of the necessity of co-operation to achieve common ends. Since all men need the same things up to a certain point, all men desire the co-operation that can alone secure them. On the positive will thus developed society rests. But it is only up to a certain point that all men need or desire the same things. Actually, men's desires not only differ, but in many ways conflict. Man, the authors say, is a perverse creature. He is self-seeking, violent, and aggressive : in spite of his recognition that co-operation is necessary, he is disposed to regard other men as rivals or as enemies. There exists a constant will to ends which are really common and consequently to co-operation. For all that, man is constantly disposed to act in a manner that tends to make co-operation inefficient or even impossible.

Hence arise two things. In the first place, the notion of what we call morality and the authors speak of as justice is developed. Alike the sense and the idea of right and

176

wrong in conduct are developed as a result of the recognition on the one hand of the need of co-operation for the common good, on the other of the fact of man's perversity. Reason recognises that certain forms of action are injurious to the community and even destructive of it. Reason proceeds to formulate general rules, or judgments, as to what is beneficial or injurious to the community, consistent or inconsistent with the general will to co-operation, in other words right or wrong. These rules, say the authors, are the formulation of what may be called Natural Law.

How far such a view as this was new at the time, I am not prepared to say. But I must point out that it strikes at the root of mediæval orthodoxy. It is the view of Machiavelli : it is, even, an approximation to the view of Hobbes. It gets rid at once of the transcendental element in ethics. It is quite strictly utilitarian. On this view right and wrong have no reference whatever to a final end of man in another life ; no necessary relation at all to any cosmic purpose. But I must add that, if we take their book as a whole, the authors do not seem to be anything like fully aware of the tremendous implications of their theory.

They proceed, however, for a time, logically. Another consequence follows on these recognitions. Natural Law, as they define it, is conceived by the authors as the only law of early society. But from its nature it demands enforcement. Action recognised as injurious must be suppressed. Such action, the authors point out, is injurious even to the offender himself, since it tends to make impossible the co-operation he himself recognises as necessary. In these conditions the constant will to common ends must needs produce coercive government.

Government is concerned, first of all, with the repression of the perverse will in man. Its primary business is to

force men to act in their own interests. In this conception there has been found an anticipation of Rousseau. I
hardly think the matter worth discussing ; but it is well
to say that all through this portion of the *Defensor* the
writer is thinking in terms of mere need and necessity.
The recognition of need involves will ; but he is thinking
of will only as something produced by need ; and he is
not thinking in terms of ' right ' at all. But even if the
thought here were exactly the same as Rousseau's that
would be an accident of no importance or significance.
To say that a mediæval thinker anticipates Rousseau, as
though that were a compliment to the mediæval, seems
to me slightly absurd. Why not congratulate Rousseau
on having unwittingly reproduced conceptions of the
fourteenth century ? In saying this I am, I suppose,
challenging some sort of notion of progress. I would
challenge it more definitely if I knew exactly what it is.

Government, then, according to the *Defensor*, comes into
existence owing to the felt need of repressing activities
injurious to society. But there is another reason for
the existence of government. The final end of political
society, the authors say, may be stated as the realisation
of *tranquillitas*. This term is explained only gradually.
Tranquillitas involves or includes, first of all, a condition
of peace and security within the community. Such security
is the condition of all prosperity and of all progress. Quite
distinctly the authors contemplate progress. Where peace
is, they say, there " intellectual capacities increase and moral
activities improve as humankind multiplies, generation
by generation." For all that, the end of society is not
mere peace and security. The State is a co-operative
association for securing common ends. Perfect *tranquillitas* involves a perfect adjustment of the means to the

ends, a perfect co-operation in which there is neither waste nor friction. Government, therefore, is required not only for the repression of perversity but for the organisation of co-operation.

The conception is illuminated by an analysis of the functions necessary to general well-being. They are definitely described and enumerated. There is the function of the judge and that of the soldier. The soldier, it is remarked, is needed to defend the community against attack from outside. There is the function of the farmer : the business of agriculture and the provision of food. There is the function of the artificer : the business of making needful things, houses, clothing, tools, and so forth. There is the function of the capitalist (*pars pecuniativa*), who exists to keep the labourer going. Lastly, there is the highly peculiar function of the priest, which is dealt with later. All these are to be so organised and co-ordinated that, each subserving the common ends, there shall be no waste anywhere of time or of labour. There must not be too many artificers or too many soldiers. It is the business of government to allot to each man his proper work and keep him at it.

The conception is, it may be said, quite what we call socialistic. But what may need pointing out is, that it seems to imply that the end of the State is material prosperity. At all events, all the needs subserved by government are, with one exception, needs that arise simply from the conditions of man's life on earth.

But there is the one exception. What is the priest doing in this galley ? The writer himself puts the question. The necessity of all the other functions enumerated is, he says, perfectly evident : but there is no evident necessity for the priest. Yet everywhere, in all societies, religion and some kind of ecclesiastical organisation have existed. He puts it as a puzzling question, why this should be so. Logically, I think, the writer's thought bound him to deny that the priest was in any sense necessary. Perhaps he was not conscious of this : perhaps he dared not go so far. But he does go one step farther toward such an elimination. He makes a remarkable suggestion. Governmental control of man's perversity is limited and inadequate. There is much objectionable activity that cannot be detected and much that can hardly be reached by law at all. From this fact, he suggests, arose religion and the priest. " Legislators have, therefore, imagined a God, from whom nothing is concealed and who commands the observance of the law under penalties." The true function of the priest, in fact, is to supplement the action of police and judge by the fear of Hell. The suggestion is outrageously crude : but there it is. No sooner has he made it, however, than he nullifies it. He goes on, hastily, to say that " the right view of God and the future life and the priesthood came only with Christianity." What was the man's real thought ? Can he have believed that Christianity formed a solitary exception to his devastating generalisation ? Was he merely trying to emphasise his notion that the position of the priest in society is justified by police necessities ? I do not know. The whole question is dropped and never referred to again.

We have reached, then, this point : that, whatever may be the explanation of the priest in general, the Christian revelation must be accepted. How much does this involve ? The Christian revelation informs us that there is a future life, and that well-being in that future depends upon acceptance of the beliefs, and observance of the rules, imposed by the revelation. Those rules include the

sacramental system of the Church ; and the priest therefore
becomes necessary to salvation. This being so, men will
not be content without such assurance of salvation as may
be possible. The greatest good of society will include this
assurance. The secular authority must, therefore, recognise and maintain the Christian Church. But no more than
this is involved. The activities of the priest have reference
only to welfare in another world, except so far as, incidentally, they assist in the repression of perversity. The
priest has no possible claim to interfere with the co-operative
effort to secure earthly ends. His function is, simply,
to give instruction in the requisites of salvation, to exhort
and to warn and to administer sacraments. The writer
sees no need of any sort of ecclesiastical organisation independent of, or even separate from, that of the State. He
does not, in this connexion, even mention the Pope. All
that he concedes is the usefulness of the priest.

From this we pass to a discussion of the constitution
of the government that has been shown to be necessary.
Fundamental in this consideration is the conception of
law and of how law comes to be. Law, it is declared, is
essentially a judgment as to what is just and advantageous
to the community. It is an imperative expression of the
common need, formulated by reason, promulgated by
recognised authority, sanctioned by force. Just because
it is this, the Legislator must needs be either the whole
community or its *valentior pars*. This last term is never
defined. It seems, ordinarily, to be used by the authors
to signify a numerical majority : but I doubt whether they
intended absolutely to commit themselves to this. Perhaps the ambiguous phrase 'effective majority' might cover
their meaning. In any case, by *valentior pars* they certainly
did not mean any particular or possible aristocratic class.

They declare against class government quite explicitly. They seem to have thought that, normally at least, the *valentior pars* would be the numerical majority.

The community or its *valentior pars* is, they assert, and under all conditions must be, the Legislator. No theory of right is involved : there is no question of right here at all. They are simply stating what seems to them a fact. They are aware that, ordinarily, the community as a whole is powerless to initiate legislation. It may delegate its law-making power to others, and in a large community it must do so. But the fact that the people is the Legislator can in no way be altered.

To be perfectly operative, it is declared, law must be universally willed. In a state of perfect *tranquillitas* it, presumably, would be. Actually it is not so. What the writer is saying appears to amount to this : that law is not made by enactment, but by obedience. Law must be recognised as expressing a common need ; and only so far as it is so recognised will it be obeyed. The writer does not say that to impose upon a community law that does not correspond to its needs is tyrannical or wicked ; he says it is impossible. The community makes law by obeying law.

The exact form of the government is conceived, not as in any sense a matter of right, but as a matter of expediency in relation to circumstance. Different forms, it is said, have existed in different times and places ; and it is clearly implied that the best form at one time and place need not be the best at another. It is suggested that formal legislative power would best be exercised by an elected assembly. Certainly it ought not to lie with any particular class or section ; for in no such class will the general will to the common good predominate. But it is not suggested that this mode of realising legislative power is always and necessarily best. It is suggested, even, that legislative power may be delegated to the executive government, the *pars principans* itself. No arrangement that can be made will alter the fact that the community is the Legislator.

Now as to the *pars principans*. It is the executive organ of the community, the agent of the Legislator. Well-ordered government is government " in the common interests of all, in accordance with the will of the subject." It is this will that the *pars principans* represents. It has no power or right that is not derived from the Legislator, and by the Legislator it can at all times be deprived of all power and right. Yet all legal and formal power may be delegated to it. The extent of the delegation does not alter its nature. The condition of the very existence of the *pars principans* is that it should govern in the general interest and by the general will. It may take any form ; but it is argued that the best form executive government can take is, ordinarily, that of an elective monarchy.

The theory of the community as Legislator, as it appears in the *Defensor*, is, it seems to me, difficult to understand ; and I must confess that I do not feel perfectly sure that I have presented the thought quite rightly. But it does certainly seem to me that the *Defensor* contains no plea for what we call parliamentary government or for any particular form of government at all. Nor can I trace any connexion between its thought and the republicanism of Italian cities. Padua itself can hardly be said to have been a republic in 1324 ; but no doubt a republican tradition existed there and may have been dear to Marsilio. If so the fact does not appear in the *Defensor*. Its authors show a preference for elective monarchy and an elected legislature. One can say no more than that.

All this is from Part I of the *Defensor*. So far as the book contains a theory of the nature of political society, this is set forth only in Part I. It is, in fact, a logically coherent conception : a statement as to the nature of political society, wherever and in whatever form it may exist. The argument is severely abstract and the reasoning close. The writer refers constantly to Aristotle. On the other hand, he refers to the Scriptures only, I think, in one passage : and that passage is the one irrelevancy in the argument.

With Part III of the book I need not deal here : it adds nothing of much importance. Part II is devoted to an attack upon the actual Church and its claims. In the very first chapter of the book we are told that Aristotle has analysed and stated all the causes of *intranquillitas* save one. That one has arisen since the time of Aristotle ; and it is the most dangerous of all. It consists in an *opinio perversa* as to the position and nature of the Christian Church. This malignant error, expressed in papal bulls, threatens all states with destruction and must itself be exposed and destroyed. Its exposure is the object of Part II.

The authors do not, it must be said, show any real understanding of the position they are attacking. They do not even attempt to state it. They attack it not in its essential contentions but in its detailed applications. They set out, in Part II, to prove four things : (1) that the Church as such has no rightful or rational claim to any kind of coercive jurisdiction ; (2) that the clergy as such have no claim to any kind of immunity from, or independence of, secular jurisdiction ; (3) that neither Pope nor clergy have any right to govern or even to speak for the Church ; (4) that the clergy have no rightful title to property. They try to prove these propositions largely by reference to Scripture. On their own showing, out of their own mouths, as it were, Pope and clergy are to be convicted of imposture and usurpation.

Here, for the first time, we come upon incoherence. In Part I there was no question at all of the exercise of any coercive jurisdiction by the clergy, nor was there any question of Church government as such. The difficulty, in Part I, had been to find any justification at all for the existence of the Church. If the view set forth in Part I were valid the questions dealt with in Part II could not arise. All that the authors had now to do was to show that, given the conclusions already arrived at, the claims of the Pope were preposterous. But they do not even attempt to do this. The argument of Part II is but slightly connected with the conclusions of Part I. The admissions made in Part II are not really consistent with the view set forth earlier. I must add that in the later parts of the book the logical arrangement and severe abstraction of Part I disappear altogether. We are dealing, now, with actual claims and with Scripture ; and we deal with them in no logical order and with much rhetoric and rancour. The argument is continually interrupted by irrelevant diatribes against Pope and clergy.

It is impossible, indeed, to take the argument of Part II very seriously. It proceeds, mainly, on two assertions. In the first place, it is declared that the case for the Pope rests on a fundamental error. He, it is said, in bull and decretal, habitually uses the term ' the Church ' to signify the clergy alone. But the Church does not consist of the clergy : the Church is the *universitas fidelium*. All true believers are members of the Church ; all true believers are, in truth, ecclesiastics. The language reminds one of Luther; but the writer does not mean what Luther meant. When he says that every true Christian is *vir ecclesiasticus* he means that every Christian is a member of the legislative body of the Church. If, at least, there be a Legislator in relation to spiritual things, every true believer is a member of it.

But what are spiritual things? Here we come to what I take to be the other main proposition of Part II. " Temporal," it is declared, are all things that have their origin and being in time. With none of these is the Church concerned. Such a definition makes any definition of spiritual things difficult. But the writer did not quite see the difficulty. " Spiritual " things, he says, are incorporeal; they are mere mental activities untranslated into act; or, if there be any acts which are spiritual, they are such as relate only to another life. He gives fasting as an instance. But he makes his main point quite clear. The clergy are no more spiritual than other people. They are temporal things—their bodies and their acts and their property.

From these premises all the propositions which the authors chiefly wished to prove, with the exception of that concerning Church property, might have been shown to follow. But this is not quite the actual procedure. The clergy appeal to the Scriptures : to the Scriptures they shall go. It is sought to show that no ground exists in Scripture for the claim of the clergy or of the Church, in any sense, to coercive jurisdiction : that, equally, no ground exists for any claim by the clergy to special immunities. It must have given our Paduan immense satisfaction to use scriptural texts as rods for the clerical back.

The argument as to clerical property had, of course, very important practical bearings. But, as an argument, it is preposterous. It begins with a definition of property that might have been learned at Bologna or Montpellier or Orléans. Ownership, it is laid down, is a right defensible by an action at law. It is a strictly legal right, created by secular authority. It is, simply, a legal fact. Have the clergy any right to claim or defend property by actions at law? Such actions, it is asserted, were forbidden by the Fathers to the " perfect." The words, " If thou wilt be perfect, sell that thou hast and give to the poor," are quoted. Now, professionally, the clergy are the perfect: and the conclusion is obvious. Whether they actually like it or not, the clergy, for their own sakes, should be relieved of compromising and entangling worldly possessions. One cannot help thinking that along with all this went a sardonic grin. But the grin is lost to us, hidden behind the veil of the Latin.

The clergy have no more than a claim to maintenance. To whom, then, does clerical property belong? The answer given is a little confused. It belongs to the Legislator, " or to such person or persons as are delegated by it, or to those who dedicated the property—that is, the patrons of churches." The meaning seems to be that, unless some private patron can make good a claim, the property belongs to the community and may be disposed of by the secular government. Tithe is expressly included.

Yet another conclusion of great practical importance is reached. An ecclesiastical benefice is a temporal thing, and in fact a form of property. The secular authority cannot, it is admitted, make a priest. Priesthood is created only by ordination. Ordination confers certain powers : but it is for the secular authority to determine when and where these powers shall be actually exercised, for this is a purely temporal concern. The right of appointing to ecclesiastical

benefice in no sense belongs to the Church. The same
principle holds here as with regard to property. If no
private patron can prove a right, the right belongs to
the Legislator or its representative.

For all this, and indeed because of all this, admissions
have been made that were not made in Part I. After all,
it appears, there does exist something called the Church,
which has authority in spiritual matters. It has authority
to declare and define the faith necessary to salvation, and
therefore to define heresy. It cannot, of course, punish
the heretic; for earthly punishment, as a temporal thing,
lies wholly within the power of the Legislator. But
though it can neither punish nor compel the secular
authority to punish, it can excommunicate. All this is
admitted. The Church that has this authority has been
defined as the *universitas fidelium*. Has this community
of the faithful a voice? Has it any means of expression
at all?

At this point the authors of the *Defensor* hesitate. When
they declared that, putting aside the rights of private
patrons, it was for the secular authority to appoint to
benefice, they must surely have been thinking of a system
of localised churches within localised states. They can
hardly have meant to make the practically absurd suggestion that such power should be everywhere vested in the
Emperor. But, apparently, they were not prepared to
assert definitely that the Universal Church could have no
means of expression. They proceed to attribute to it a
means of expressing its judgments.

They admit that the Church has a voice; but they
emphatically deny that the Pope is the voice of the Church.
There is a long argument to the effect that the Pope's
claim is founded on misinterpretations of Scripture and on

mere fables. St Peter was not given any special authority, and, even if he were, he was probably never at Rome : and so forth. At most they admit that the Pope owns a titular, decorative, and symbolic headship of the clergy.

The Legislator in spiritual matters is the *universitas fidelium*. It cannot act as a mass meeting. It can act, it is declared, only through an elected body, which must represent the laity as well as the clergy. To this General Council and to it alone belongs authority to declare doctrine and define heresy and to excommunicate. It can depose and elect the Pope. It can indeed, it is said, with flagrant inconsistency, appoint to all ecclesiastical benefices.

How is this General Council of the Church to be summoned and how exactly is it to be composed ? The Pope is not to summon it, though he may be allowed, formally and without special powers, to preside at its deliberations. It is for the secular governments of Christendom to summon the Council ; and it is for them also to determine the exact mode of its election. At most the Pope may be permitted to call upon the secular authorities to issue a summons ; but he cannot in any way bind them to do so.

Let no one suppose for a moment that the authors of the *Defensor* were dreaming of a reform of the Church, or that they desired to substitute government of the Church by General Councils for the government of the Pope. It is manifest that they desired no such thing. They felt bound, apparently, to allow a voice to the Universal Church ; and they gave it a voice that was very unlikely ever to say a word. It must have been clear to them that no such Council as this of their devising was likely ever to meet. They must have seen that, if ever it did meet, it would represent the wishes of the secular governments and very little, if anything, else. They have so cleverly arranged things that the Pope is left in vacancy and the Church with a voice but no utterance. There is no real power left to determine what heresy is, no real power to excommunicate. There is nothing left to prevent the secular authorities from taking over all ecclesiastical appointments and disposing as they please of Church property, since nothing but a General Council of their own summons and construction can interfere or overrule them. The Church, as an organised, authoritative body, is abolished in all but name.

The fame of the *Defensor*, both in the fourteenth century and later, rested, I think, upon Part II. What attracted attention, what roused the fury of the Pope and gratified alike the Emperor of the fourteenth century and Protestants in the sixteenth, was its uncompromising onslaught on papal and clerical claims and on clerical property. But any claim the book has to be regarded as the work of a great thinker must rest upon Part I. Part II is vigorous, bold, animated and ingenious, and, I fancy, grimly humorous. But its argumentation is poor and often, I think, insincere. It is full of irrelevance and claptrap. But the thought of Part I, in spite of its ambiguities and its partial failure in expression, does, it seems to me, go deep and reach far. Whether the coupling with it of the term ' secularism ' be justified or no I must leave to the reader. The point is not worth pressing. But I will add a few words as to the careers of its reputed authors after the completion of their book. Both went together to the court of the Emperor Ludwig and were welcomed by him and made much of. The Emperor himself had been excommunicated by the Pope only a short time before. In 1327 Ludwig went to Italy and his two literary champions went with him. In January 1328 he entered Rome.

MARSILIO OF PADUA

Marsilio was made Imperial Vicar in the city and, governing Rome for the Emperor, employed himself in harrying the clergy who dared to obey the papal interdict. He acquired, it seems, quite a reputation for cruelty : a thing, perhaps, not easy to do in fourteenth-century Italy. John of Jandun was appointed, by the Emperor, Bishop of Ferrata ; but he died on his journey to possession. Forced to leave Rome, Ludwig returned to Germany and Marsilio went with him. Thenceforward he remained, apparently, in the Emperor's service and favour ; but we do not know when he died. There is no mention of him after 1342. But he must have enjoyed himself enormously at Rome.

J. W. ALLEN

BIBLIOGRAPHY

Defensor Pacis. Text in Goldast, *Monarchia S. Imperii Romani.* Also an edition in Teubner's *Quellensammlung,* ed. R. Scholz, Leipzig, 1914.

R. LABANCA : *Marsilio da Padova.*

I. CAPPA-LEGORA : *La Politica di Dante et di Marsilio da Padova.*

N. VALOIS : " Jean de Jandun et Marsile de Padoue," appendix in *Hist. litt. de la France,* tome xxxiii.

S. RIEZLER : *Die Literarischen Widersacher der Päpste zur Zeit Ludwig des Baiers.*

E. EMERTON : *The " Defensor Pacis " of Marsiglio of Padua.* Cambridge (U.S.A.), 1920.

L. STIEGLITZ : *Die Staatstheorie des Marsilius von Padua.* Teubner, 1914.

C. W. PREVITÉ-ORTON : " Marsiglio of Padua," two articles in *English Historical Review,* October 1922 and January 1923.

VIII

JOHN WYCLIFFE AND DIVINE DOMINION

I

I WISH to preface my discourse on Wycliffe with some general remarks on the course to which this lecture forms the conclusion. It will have been noted that the lectures are very unevenly distributed over the period of the Middle Ages : the duration of time which divides St Augustine from John of Salisbury is not far short of that which separates John of Salisbury from the present day. Six of the seven thinkers treated belong to the last quarter of the mediæval millennium ; between the first and the second of them yawns the dark chasm whch stretches from the fifth century to the twelfth. Now this long epoch of seven hundred years was by no means devoid of great events. It saw the establishment of the barbarian kingdoms in Western Europe ; the rise and spread of Islam ; the incursions of the vikings ; the settlement of the Magyars in Hungary ; the organisation of Christendom for discipline under Pope and priesthood, and for defence under Emperor and knighthood ; the feudalisation of society ; the wild adventure of the Crusades. It was, indeed, an epoch of intense and varied activity, of fierce energy, and of vast achievement. But it was an epoch of deeds rather than of words ; of institutions rather than of ideas. Lord Bryce has described it as " essentially unpolitical," and it was so in the sense that it was engaged in constructing states and not in formulating political theories.

192

JOHN WYCLIFFE

It is regrettable that the Middle Ages were not more articulate. They were dominated by notions so alien from our modern modes of thought that, in the absence of express statement, it is difficult for us to realise or formulate their creeds. No doubt, for example, there were political principles of some sort inherent and implicit in feudalism—ideas of suzerainty as based on contract, of the mutual responsibility of rulers and ruled, of hereditary right, of territorial dominion, of power as property. But so long as feudalism prevailed they were never made explicit. Not until feudalism had decayed and was passing away were its fundamental theories extracted, examined, classified, and systematised. The ' feudal system,' as Professor Maitland has told us, was introduced into England by Sir Henry Spelman in the seventeenth century. Similarly, I think, it might be contended that the Holy Roman Empire was established by Lord Bryce in 1864, and that the *Respublica Christiana* was invented by Father Figgis in 1910. The men of the Middle Ages did not clarify their thoughts : the majority of them had no thoughts to clarify. They lived by instinct and tradition, like the higher animals. One has to infer their motives, as M. Maeterlinck infers from observation the polity of the bees.

Soon after the passing of the millennial year (A.D. 1000), however, the inarticulate era came to an end ; silence gave place to sound. The first utterances of political significance were, it is true, more like the roars of infuriated bulls, or the screams of exasperated eagles, than the speeches of rational men : they were the alternate anathemas and blasphemies which marked the Investiture Controversy. These elemental utterances, however, unedifying as they were in themselves, stirred the mediæval mind to political speculation. They compelled attention to the problem of

N

the relation of Papacy to Empire, of spiritual to temporal authority, of Church to State. At first, the ecclesiastical theorists had it all their own way. They alone possessed such knowledge of letters as survived from classical times ; they still commanded the consciences of men. Hence the cause which they supported emerged substantially triumphant from the Investiture struggle ; the victorious Papacy increased in splendour and power until it reached its culmination of might, majesty, and dominion under the great Innocent III. The theory of papal sovereignty is well expressed and enforced by John of Salisbury and St Thomas Aquinas, as well as by others, such as St Bernard and Ægidius Romanus.

The age of St Thomas and his faithful henchman Ægidius was the high-water mark of mediæval Christendom. The rebellious empire of the Hohenstaufen had been destroyed : the Papacy reigned apparently supreme in all causes both spiritual and temporal. Secular philosophy had been subordinated to divine theology ; Aristotle had been made to acknowledge the overlordship of Augustine : the *Summa* of St Thomas contained the complete, unified, and harmonised corpus of human knowledge, which it was supposed would never have to be supplemented or superseded. The great thirteenth century, however, had no sooner come to an end than new revolt, disorder, heresy, schism set in. The age of assured faith, implicit obedience, disciplined activity, gave place to one of doubt, discord, and destruction. The ideal unity of Christendom was dissolved in the confusion of national states ; the vision of the peace of God faded before the reality of the strife of men. During the course of these lectures the dramatic climax of the thirteenth century and its swift-following anti-climax in the fourteenth have often been referred to. In the Jubilee of 1300 the Papacy, in the person of Boniface VIII, appeared to touch heights of imperial power never attained before. In 1303 the tragedy of Anagni, with its sequel of confusion, compromise, and captivity, revealed the deceptiveness of the appearance, and displayed the true impotence of the Papacy in temporal concerns. The Papal Monarchy was at an end ; the effort of the Church to unify and govern the world had failed ; the nations and their kings had refused to follow the way of peace which St Thomas Aquinas had marked out for them.

The problem of the fourteenth century was how to restore tranquillity to the distracted and demoralised fragments of what had lately been Christendom. We have seen how Dante saw the one and only way of hope in the reunion of Christendom under the Holy Roman Emperor ; how Pierre Du Bois, perceiving that the mediæval Empire had passed away even more irrevocably than the mediæval Papacy, urged a reconstruction of Christendom under the most potent of its rulers, the king of France ; how Marsilio of Padua, wholly rejecting the idea of any reunion or reconstruction of the Church-state of the Middle Ages, looked forward to the establishment of a Peace of the People. We have now to inquire how John Wycliffe envisaged the problem of his time, and what were the political ideas which seemed to him to point the way to peace and progress.

II

Wycliffe was born in the north of England about the year 1320. As he grew up to manhood, the evils which had marked the opening of the fourteenth century became manifestly worse. In particular, the Papacy, exiled from Rome and established at Avignon (1309–76), having been robbed of its temporal suzerainty, lost also its spirituality, and sank into a deplorable condition of religious apathy, moral corruption, and intellectual contempt. It also passed under the control of its destroyer, the king of France, and seemed to be degraded to the ignominious position of a mere tool of his policy. At the same time its departure from Italy involved the loss of the revenues of the Papal States, and this necessitated a formidable increase in the demands for money made upon the faithful in northern lands. England, in particular, which had been recognised as a fief of the Papacy by King John, was drawn upon heavily to support the growing expenses of the papal court : French cardinals became the absentee holders of the richest English benefices ; curial agents collected in this country for the advantage of Avignon a larger sum than flowed into the coffers of the king himself.[1] The exasperation which in any circumstances would have been caused by the loss of English patronage and the drain of English wealth was incalculably aggravated when the Hundred Years War broke out (1337). From that time onward it was felt that the papal overlord of England was the pliable dependent of England's most deadly foe ; and that the ecclesiastical treasure of the nation was being prostituted to the comfort and encouragement of the enemy.

In the midst of these disaffections and discontents fell

---

[1] " At Salisbury in 1326 the dean, the precentor, the treasurer, two arch-deacons, and twenty-three prebendaries, were papal nominees " (Capes, *English Church*, p. 86). Fifty years later " The income of the French clergy alone accruing from English livings was estimated at £60,000 a year " (Lechler, *John Wycliffe*, p. 168). Absentee French cardinals held the deaneries of York, Carlisle, and Lincoln ; the archdeaconries of Canterbury, Durham, Suffolk, and York ; besides many prebends and other benefices (Lewis, *John Wicliffe*, p. 34).

the Black Death (1349). This colossal catastrophe, which
so well-informed a historian as Professor Thorold Rogers
regarded as the most momentous event recorded in English
history, had a profound and far-reaching effect in the religious
sphere, as well as in the spheres of politics, economics,
and society. It shook the ecclesiastical system to its
foundation. It destroyed the faith of the common man in
the efficacy of prayer, in the virtue of priestly ministrations,
in the benefits of pilgrimages and penances, in the value of
piety and the worth of good deeds. A blind, cruel, and
irresistible Fate seemed to sweep away good and bad
indifferently to a single swift and abominable doom. To
the religious man it raised problems which had slumbered
since the days when Augustine had sought to solve the
mystery of the agony in which the old Roman world was
perishing. Was man in any sense the arbiter of his own
destiny ? Was there such a thing as free will ? Was
not the whole course of every creature, both in this world
and the next, foreknown and foreordained from the beginning ? Were not the pretences of the priests to affect
the welfare of any body, or the fate of any soul, by means
of masses, absolutions, penances, fastings, and the like,
palpable absurdities and execrable frauds ? These were
questions, and this was a temper, that went far deeper into
the abysses of doubt than those which merely concerned
papal patronage, or ecclesiastical jurisdiction, or the
revenues of an alien hierarchy. While the new spirit of
national patriotism menaced the temporalities of the
Papacy, the revival of the Augustinian conception of the
Church as the community of the predestined elect laid
an axe to the root of the spiritual claims of the mediæval
priesthood, and prepared the ground for the growth of
Lollardy and Calvinism. Such were the circumstances in

the midst of which Wycliffe grew up. It was an age wherein an old order was visibly breaking up. What part did Wycliffe play in either discerning or determining the lines along which the new order would frame itself?

III

Into the details of Wycliffe's life it is not necessary to enter here. Many of them still remain obscure,[1] owing partly to the fact that the reformer had not sufficient personal fascination to make men wish to remember much about him,[2] and partly to the fact that the destructive inquisition of the later mediæval clergy went far to obliterate all traces of his abhorred activity. The sixty-odd years of his earthly span can be divided into four periods as follows: (1) his juvenile career, c. 1320–35; (2) his academic career, 1335–74; (3) his political career, 1374–78; and (4) his anti-papal career, 1378–84.

Neither the exact date nor the precise place of his birth can be determined with certainty; but evidence seems to point to the year 1320 and to Spresswell, near Old Richmond, in the North Riding of Yorkshire.[3] Of his parentage, his home life, and his early education nothing is known; but it is probable that he lived and learned somewhere in the valley of the Tees, until, about 1335, he was enrolled as a member of Balliol College, Oxford. Balliol was the college of the Northerners: it stood for Teutonism as against Latinism; for national independence as against the ultramontane cosmopolitanism of the *Respublica*

---

[1] It is reported that at a recent examination the only thing about which one of the candidates was quite certain was that Wycliffe was "the editor of the *Morning Star*"!

[2] We have no record of any friendships of his. Among his numerous writings not a single letter is to be found.

[3] See discussion in Lechler's *John Wycliffe*, pp. 79–84.

Christiana ; for the realism of Duns Scotus as against the prevailing nominalism of William of Ockham. Its great rival and antagonist was Merton, the college of the Southerners, the champion of *sacerdotium*, universalism, and tradition. All Wycliffe's associations were with Balliol ; his spirit was the Balliol spirit ; his attitude throughout life the Balliol attitude. He rose to be Master of the college in 1361 —the first sure date we have in his recorded biography. Much complication has been caused by the fact that the name ' John Wycliffe ' (spelled variously) has been found in the contemporary registers of both Merton College and Queen's College. The older biographers of Wycliffe tried to fit all the entries into the story of the reformer's life : the result was chaos and hopeless perplexity. The recent researches, however, of Mr Courthope, Dr Reginald Lane Poole, Dr Hastings Rashdall, and others, have made abundantly clear the curious fact that in the middle of the fourteenth century there were no less than three persons of the same name resident simultaneously in the university. One was the reformer ; the second was a Fellow of Merton College who for a brief period was Warden of Canterbury Hall and who finally died Prebendary of Chichester and Rector of Horsted Keynes in Sussex in 1383 ; the third was an obscure almonry boy of Queen's College, known only as a renter of rooms in the college, and as a person who omitted to pay his debts. It is eminently satisfactory and disembarrassing to have got the reformer clear of both the obscurantism of the Merton Wycliffe and the insolvency of his namesake at Queen's. For Wycliffe, as we have already remarked, was essentially a Balliol man. Now to be essentially a Balliol man is to be portentous. The typical Scholar of Balliol is a youth distinguished by ominous brilliance ; the typical Fellow of

Balliol is a meteor of high magnitude ; the typical Master of Balliol—well, Wycliffe was the typical Master of Balliol, luridly luminous, heretically vaporous, the Great Nebula itself in the constellation of Lucifer.

In Oxford, during the forty years of his association with the university, Wycliffe rose to a position of the highest eminence. Even his enemy, Henry de Knyghton, acknowledged that " in philosophy he was reckoned as inferior to none, and as unequalled in the exercises of the schools," and spoke of him as " a man of profound wit, exceptionally strong and effective in disputations—one who was regarded by the common sort of divines as little less than a god." One of the severest of his modern critics similarly admits that he was " the leading figure in the academic circles of his day ; one of the last of the great schoolmen." [1] He was " the Evangelical Doctor," the teacher who increasingly tended to bring all things to the test of the Gospel, until finally, at the end of a long and painful evolution, he proclaimed the Scriptures as interpreted by human reason to be the supreme standard of verity. He was not an original thinker : he followed Plato in his exaltation of Ideas ; Augustine in his conception of the Church ; Grosseteste (whom he considered a greater man than Aristotle [2]) in his antagonism to the Papacy ; Bradwardine in his leaning toward predestination ; Ockham in his insistence on priestly poverty ; Fitzralph in his theory of dominion. What *was* original in him was the intellectual fearlessness which pushed premises to their logical conclusion, the rationalism which refused to bow to authority, and the moral courage which defied the terrors

[1] W. W. Capes, *The English Church in the Fourteenth and Fifteenth Centuries*, p. 110.
[2] " Plato, Augustinus, Lincolniensis, sunt longe clariores philosophi."

of the Inquisition. It is noteworthy that all through the academic period of his career, and indeed to within three years of his death, he carried the university with him. He was regarded by doctors and scholars alike as the champion of the freedom of the *studium* against the mortifying restraints of the *sacerdotium* ; as the exponent of the claims of philosophy against the ascendancy of theology ; as a defender of the rights of the secular clergy against the encroachments of monks and friars ; above all, as the invincible maintainer of a lofty realism against the decadent nominalism of the rival University of Paris. This reputation became wide as Christendom itself, and he, more than anyone else, gave to Oxford the intellectual glory of this its Golden Age. It was unfortunate for Oxford that the liberty which she enjoyed in the middle of the fourteenth century should have become associated with deadly heresy on Wycliffe's part, with Lollard schism, with the Peasants' Revolt, and with world-disorder generally. For these things made it possible for Archbishop Courtenay to establish in 1382 an Inquisition which effectively stifled freedom of thought. From that date Oxford ceased to be the national centre of progressive ideas ; she became, what she has since remained, " the home of lost causes and impossible beliefs."

IV

To return to Wycliffe. During the years when he was teaching philosophy at Oxford stirring events were transpiring in the larger world. In particular, the Hundred Years War was running its evil and lamentable course, involving the English nation in ever-widening circles of animosities. Among these animosities the most serious was that which sundered England from the Papacy. The

Papacy had been growing in unpopularity throughout England ever since that fatal year, 1213, when Innocent III had extorted from the renegade King John a recognition of the papal suzerainty over his realm. The increasing claims to jurisdiction and the insatiable demands for money which resulted from John's surrender had roused a swelling indignation among the people. The annual tribute of 1000 marks (700 for the kingdom of England, 300 for the lordship of Ireland) which John had agreed to pay to the papal court as a symbol of his submission was frequently withheld after 1272, and in 1333 was wholly suspended. In 1343 Parliament petitioned the King against papal provisions, and in 1351 passed the Statute of Provisors. The year 1353 saw the first Statute of Præmunire, designed to restrict foreign jurisdictions in England ; in 1365 this general statute was pointed by another which expressly prohibited the carrying of suits to papal courts. This direct challenge roused Pope Urban V to action : he demanded payment of the tribute, together with arrears due since 1333. A special Parliament was called by Edward III to deal with this demand. It met in May 1366, and after due deliberation rejected the papal claim on the ground that John's surrender, with its attendant promise, was *ultra vires* and in violation of his coronation oath. Urban V felt it inadvisable to press the matter farther in face of the strenuous national resistance. Not so, however, his successor, Gregory XI, eight years later.[1]

In 1374, when the papal demand for the tribute (with its implication of feudal dependence) was renewed, the position of England was appreciably weaker. On the one hand, the nation was no longer united : a formidable conflict was raging between a clerical party, headed by

---

[1] See the continuation of *Eulogium Historiarum*, iii, 337.

William of Wykeham, and an anti-clerical party, headed
by John of Gaunt, Duke of Lancaster and son of King
Edward III. On the other hand, the French were recover-
ing victory in the great war, and were rapidly driving
the English out of their land. In these circumstances, the
Papacy, with French support, resumed the practice of
provisions, ignored the prohibitions of *præmunire*, and
redemanded the Johannine tribute. The once glorious
King of England, hero of Crécy and Poictiers, now rapidly
sinking into senile incompetence, was eager for tranquillity
on almost any terms. Hence in 1374 he sent two missions
to Bruges, one, under John of Gaunt, to treat of a truce
with the French ; the other, under the Bishop of Bangor,
to reach an accommodation with the Papacy. With the
Bishop of Bangor went John Wycliffe. This event probably
marks his first emergence from academic into political life.

Neither of the two missions of 1374 achieved any
conspicuous success. We are not now concerned with
the humiliating terms which the Duke of Lancaster had
to accept from the French king. As to the Bishop of
Bangor's business, so little did he press the matter of provisors, and so agreeable did he make himself to the papal
representatives, that on his return to England he was at
once ' provided ' by the Pope with a more lucrative bishopric
than the one he held ! The question of the tribute and
its feudal implication was, however, better managed.
This, apparently, was Wycliffe's special concern. He
had made himself master of both the law and the philosophy
inherent in the idea of dominion, and he put up an un-
answerable case against the papal overlordship. Behind
his logic, moreover, making it doubly effective, was the
passionate resolve of the English nation not to admit its
political subjection to the court of Avignon—which was

regarded as itself subject to the king of France. Wycliffe's arguments against the feudal dominion of the Papacy over England are summarised in a document entitled *Determinatio quædam Magistri Johannis Wyclif de Dominio contra unum Monachum*—a document to which Dr Loserth conclusively assigns a date subsequent to 1374.[1] It appears that a certain monk—probably William Wadford, the opponent with whom Wycliffe crossed swords in his *De Ecclesia* and his *De Civili Dominio*—had had the temerity to support the papal claim to feudal suzerainty over England, and to contend that, as the Pope had conferred the government of England upon the king on condition of the payment of the annual tribute, and as the tribute had ceased to be paid, the king had forfeited his title to the crown. Wycliffe, as the expert on this problem of dominion, was commissioned to answer the audacious ecclesiastic. He did so in this remarkable *Determinatio*, wherein he describes himself as *peculiaris regis clericus talis qualis*—a curious expression which probably means no more than that he had been the King's representative at Bruges in 1374. The *Determinatio* is constructed in the form of a series of speeches delivered in Parliament by seven lords.[2] At one time it was thought to be a veracious report—the earliest extant—of a genuine parliamentary debate. It is, however, too good to be true. It is too logical for lords ; too consecutive and coherent ; too free from tautology and irrelevance. It resembles those admirable eighteenth-century parlia-

---

[1] Loserth, in *English Historical Review*, April 1896. The document itself is printed, not very correctly however, by Lewis in his *John Wicliffe* (1720), pp. 363–371. Emendations in the text are made by F. D. Matthew, *English Works of Wyclif* (1880), p. v. Summaries of the arguments will be found in R. Vaughan's *Tracts and Treatises of John de Wycliffe* (1845), pp. xix–xxiv, and in G. Lechler's *John Wycliffe* (1884), pp. 124–130.

[2] " Primo ergo transmitto doctorem meum reverendum ad solutionem hujus argumenti quam audivi in quodam consilio a dominis secularibus esse datam."

mentary reports which Dr Johnson wrote after he had been sound asleep during the whole evening, when (having escaped the distraction of the speeches) he woke up refreshed and full of lusty resolve that the Whig dogs should not have the best of the argument. The *Determinatio* is Wycliffe pure and undiluted. The seven secular lords are but a ghostly body-guard arrayed before him in the hope of averting from himself the dreadful thunderbolt of papal excommunication. He was not yet a rebel against the Papacy ; he had not yet challenged any article of the Catholic faith ; he still (in this very document) described himself as *humilis et obedientialis filius Romanæ Ecclesiæ*.

The arguments advanced against the papal suzerainty were briefly these : first, the kingdom of England had been obtained by conquest and not by papal grant ; secondly, feudal relations were mutual, the lord was bound to protect his vassal, and the Pope gave the king of England no such protection ; thirdly, so far was he from protecting him that he actually fostered and encouraged his mortal enemies ; but fourthly, so vast were the estates of the Church in England that the Pope was rather the sub-tenant of the king than his suzerain ; fifthly, if the Pope pardoned John in 1213 in consideration of his promise to pay 700 marks a year he was guilty of simony ; sixthly, 700 marks was an absurdly inadequate sum for a fief so magnificent as the kingdom of England ; finally, John had no right or power to pledge his monarchy, or to surrender its independence. This utterance is obviously that of the *peculiaris regis clericus* rather than of the *filius Romanæ Ecclesiæ*, and when he followed it up by formal and formidable dissertations *De Dominio Divino* and *De Civili Dominio* he could not possibly hope to escape papal censure and episcopal condemnation. No camouflage of secular lords could conceal or protect his irreverent and revolutionary head. From covertly denying the particular papal claim to lordship over England he had gone on to assail the whole system under which religious men exercised temporal power and possessed mundane property. This general attack on ecclesiastical politicians and clerical wealth excited immense interest. It was an assault led, not by an obscure fanatic like John Ball, but by the foremost schoolman of the age. It was couched, not in wild vernacular tirades, but in the ponderous logic of the latest and most approved academic Latin. It commanded attention, and it demanded energetic repulse. Its menace to the hierarchy was all the more formidable because, although Wycliffe's theory of dominion was unintelligible to the multitude, his denunciations of the worldliness and wealth of the clergy were greeted with the warmest approval by the party of John of Gaunt, by the majority of the Parliament, and by the commonalty generally. Hence in 1377 it was necessary for the Church to act, and to act with decisive vigour.

V

The year 1377—the year of Edward III's death and Richard II's accession—was the culminating point of Wycliffe's career. He was at the height of his powers. He had not as yet broken with the Church or committed himself to either heresy or schism. He was the idol of Oxford University, the hero of London City, the *protégé* of the Duke of Lancaster, the adviser of the House of Commons, and even the ally of the friars in their advocacy of apostolic poverty. So strong was his position that the first attempt to silence him entirely failed. It was made in February

206

1377 by the masterful and inquisitorial Courtenay, Bishop of London, who summoned him to appear in the cathedral church of St Paul, in order to answer for his anti-clerical teachings. He duly came, but he brought with him not only friars of the four orders to assist him in his arguments, but also the Duke of Lancaster and the Earl Marshall with a company of armed men to guard him from perils more imminent than failure in debate. The sacred court speedily became a scene of furious wrangling, in which the fiery bishop and the impious duke were the protagonists. It broke up in wild disorder before ever its cause of convocation had been so much as stated. Wycliffe, who seems to have been a passive spectator of the unseemly brawl, was conveyed into safety by his anomalous friends.

The second attack came from the Papacy itself. No doubt it had been inspired by the clerical party in England ; but apparently not by either Courtenay of London or Sudbury of Canterbury, for both were roundly rebuked for slackness in dealing with this dangerous rebel. On May 22, 1377, Pope Gregory XI (lately returned to Rome from Avignon) issued no less than five bulls directed against Wycliffe, who was accused of reviving and disseminating the perverse opinions and unlearned doctrine of Marsilio of Padua, *damnatæ memoriæ*, and his collaborator, John of Jandun. Three of the five bulls were addressed to the prelates of Canterbury and London. They provided them with three different courses of action. According as circumstances suggested, they were authorised and commanded to arrest and imprison Wycliffe ; or to get the King to do so ; or to cite him to appear at Rome. The situation was evidently a delicate one : the anti-clerical party was strong and vigilant, and the penalties of *præmunire* were not to be lightly incurred. The fourth of the bulls was addressed to the King : it exhorted him to aid the bishops in their pious task. The fifth was directed to the delinquent University of Oxford : it sternly rebuked the Chancellor and his Fellows for permitting tares to grow amid the pure wheat of their doctrine, and ordered them, on pain of the loss of their privilege, to extirpate the pernicious vegetation, and to hand over the sowers of it to the papal commissioners, viz., the Archbishop of Canterbury and the Bishop of London.[1]

Accompanying the bulls was a list of nineteen articles (reduced in subsequent recensions to eighteen) culled from Wycliffe's works and declared to be damnable. It is notable that all but one of these obnoxious propositions were derived from the treatise *De Civili Dominio*. It is further remarkable that no questions of Catholic faith were involved in them ; they referred exclusively to problems of politics, principles of property and power, relations of Church and State.[2] They were not arranged in any logical order ; they were not criticised or explained ; the grounds of their condemnation were not stated. It must be confessed that, like much of Wycliffe's writing, the meaning of some of them is extremely obscure. This much is clear, however. They exalt the State above the Church ; they subject the clergy to the judgment of the laity ; they recognise the right and proclaim the duty of secular lords

---

[1] The text of the bulls is to be found in Walsingham, *Hist. Ang.*, i, 345 *et seq.* ; also in the St Albans *Chronicon Angliæ*, p. 174 *et seq.* ; and again in the appendix to Lewis's *Wicliffe*, pp. 254–264. Summaries of their contents are given in Lechler's *Wycliffe*, pp. 162–165, and in Sergeant's *Wyclif*, pp. 175–177.

[2] For the text of the articles see Walsingham, *Hist. Ang.*, i, 353, or Lewis, *Wicliffe*, pp. 266–267. Compare also Shirley, *Fasciculi Zizaniorum*, p. 484. Lewis translates the articles with comments, pp. 42–46 ; and he further gives, from Walsingham, a paper purporting to set forth Wycliffe's own explanation of their meaning, pp. 54–63. Summaries are provided by Lechler, pp. 165–167, and by Sergeant, pp. 177–179.

to confiscate ecclesiastical property when it is abused.[1] It
will be seen that two tremendous issues were raised by this
controversy of 1377—the one by Wycliffe himself, the other
by his opponents. On the one hand, Wycliffe called upon
the State to reform a Church corrupted by worldly power
and temporal possessions. On the other hand, in self-
defence, the menaced Church sought to introduce the papal
Inquisition into England, with power to arrest, imprison,
try, and punish those who thus assailed its prerogatives.

The five bulls and the nineteen articles probably reached
Canterbury some time in June 1377 ; but for six months
nothing was done with them. The occasion was not
auspicious for their publication. Edward III died on
June 21, and a regency was established much less disposed
than the old King had been to act as jackal to the Papacy.
In October a Parliament was called which declared itself
emphatically on Wycliffe's side. It received from Wycliffe
a paper in which he stated and defended his position.[2] It
further consulted Wycliffe respecting the lawfulness of
withholding treasure from the Pope, and when he replied
that—according to natural reason, the command of the
Gospel, and the law of conscience—it *was* lawful, it
welcomed and accepted his opinion.[3] Not until this
anti-papal Parliament was prorogued did the papal commissioners venture to act. Then, on December 18, 1377,
they sent a mandate to the University of Oxford, together

---

[1] Perhaps the three most offensive articles were No. 6, " Domini temporales
possunt legitime ac meritorie auferre bona fortunæ ab ecclesia delinquente " ;
No. 17, " Licet regibus auferre temporalia a viris ecclesiasticis ipsis abutient-
ibus habitualiter " ; and No. 19, " Ecclesiasticus imo et Romanus Pontifex
potest legitime a subditis et laicis corripi, et etiam accusari."

[2] *Libellus Magistri Johannis Wycclyff quem porrexit Parliamento regis
Ricardi contra statum Ecclesiæ.* See Shirley's edition of *Fasciculi Zizaniorum*,
pp. 245–257.

[3] *Responsio Magistri Johannis Wyccliff ad dubium infrascriptum quæsitum
ab eo per Dominum Regem Angliæ Ricardum secundum et Magnum suum
Consilium, anno regni sui primo.* See Shirley, *op. cit.*, pp. 258–271.

with the bull and the articles, ordering the university
(1) to inquire into Wycliffe's opinions, and (2) to cite him
to appear to answer for his views before the papal commissioners in St Paul's.[1] The university intensely resented
this papal and episcopal interference with its liberties, and
this attack upon its most illustrious teacher. It held the
inquiry, however, and declared its finding to be that what
Wycliffe said was true, though not very happily expressed :
his nineteen propositions are pronounced *veras esse sed
male sonare in auribus auditorum* ! With this qualified
benediction Wycliffe was sent by the university to appear
before the papal commission at St Paul's.

For some reason or other, however, the commission did
not sit at St Paul's. It sat at Lambeth ; probably because
the attitude of London was disquieting. Both populace
and government were in fact alive to the menace of the
papal Inquisition. An anonymous tract in the English
language, usually attributed to Wycliffe himself, had been
widely circulated in the city, calling upon all good Christians
to rally in defence of the conclusions of Wycliffe and the
independence of the English Church. The appeal was
effective. No sooner was the court set (early in 1378) than
it was surrounded, filled, and overawed by a howling
multitude which had poured over London Bridge and made
its way tumultuously through the Borough into the
Liberties of the Archbishop. Not only was the timid
Sudbury terrified into ineptitude, but even the haughty and
domineering Courtenay was too much scared to act. Their
discomfiture was completed when a messenger arrived from
the mother of the young King, prohibiting the court from

---

[1] For the mandate see Spelman, *Concilia*, i, 625, or Wilkins, *Concilia*, iii,
123, or Lewis's *Wicliffe*, p. 264. It will be noted that the course pursued
was not any one of the three indicated in the bulls.

pronouncing any sentence upon Wycliffe. Hence, as Walsingham indignantly tells us, the words of the two would-be inquisitors were "softer than oil, to the public loss of their own dignity, and to the damage of the Universal Church." Wycliffe was merely ordered to refrain from preaching and lecturing on the subjects embodied in the nineteen propositions before the court. Then he was allowed to go forth a free man.

The rebuff to the Papacy and its agents was a severe one. Wycliffe had been merely irritated and alienated, not in the least injured, by the feeble performances of the five bulls and of the two commissioners in charge of them. The measure of Wycliffe's immunity was no doubt also the measure of the exasperation of the baffled Sudbury and Courtenay. What next they intended to do remains in doubt; for on March 27, 1378, Pope Gregory XI died, and their commission lapsed. Wycliffe thus secured a further term of impunity. The death of Pope Gregory XI, moreover, had another important effect upon his career. It gave rise to the awful schism of the Papacy which for the next thirty-nine years (1378–1417) rent in suicidal civil war an already distracted Christendom. Before the end of 1378 there were two rival Popes, Urban VI at Rome, and Clement VII gravitating toward Avignon, engaged not in tending the sheep of the Church, but in tearing one another, anathematising one another, and calling one another 'Anti-Christ'—which was the fourteenth-century equivalent to 'Bolshevik.' Hitherto Wycliffe had been, at any rate in profession, *humilis et obedientialis filius Romanæ Ecclesiæ.* In 1378 he ceased to be such. He repudiated the Papacy, and applied to both the Popes the epithets which they were applying to one another. They became, in his increasingly lurid

211

language, " monsters," " limbs of Lucifer," " vicars of the
fiend," " men glowing with Satanic pride," " sinful idiots,"
" horrible idols." Their trains of conflicting cardinals
were described by him as " incarnate devils " and " hinges
of Satan's house."

The remaining six years of Wycliffe's life were a head-
long rush, with gathering velocity, down the steep place
of heresy into a sea of a protestantism much more profound than ever Luther's became. No sixteenth-century
reformer, indeed, ever divested himself so completely of
the whole mediæval system as did Wycliffe during this
brief delirious span. Into the details of Wycliffe's career
as a religious revolutionary we are not here called upon,
or indeed permitted, to enter. Suffice it to say that this
closing period of his life (1378–84) was one of almost
incredible activity and productivity. He poured forth
pamphlets in the vernacular; he composed massive theological treatises in Latin; he organised a translation of
the Bible; he trained a band of itinerant agitators. He
ultimately laid his axe to the root of the whole sacerdotal
overgrowth when he denied and denounced the doctrine
of transubstantiation—a doctrine (comparatively recent in
its formulation) which he attributed to the direct inspiration of the devil, after he had been let loose to deceive men
at the close of the first Christian millennium.

VI

This closing period of Wycliffe's career added very little
that is new to his social and political teaching. He was
absorbed in theological controversies and ecclesiastical
conflicts. His *Trialogus* (1382), which contains incompar-
ably the best exposition of his ultimate religious negations,

is almost silent on the doctrine of dominion and its implications, which had played so large a part in the utterances of the years when he was *peculiaris regis clericus.* Another cause, besides theological preoccupation, moreover, may have tended to keep him quiet respecting dominion. The Peasants' Revolt had broken out in 1381, and the sanguinary communism of the revolutionary boors was by many attributed to the pernicious working of the Lollard leaven, which seemed to increase in virulence as it passed from Latin into English, and from the lecture-rooms of Oxford into the hovels of the villanage.[1] Now Wycliffe, like Luther after him, was a strong believer in order and in firm authoritarian government. He did not admit that his doctrine of dominion had properly any such application as John Ball and the raging peasants gave to it. But he recognised that it was difficult to safeguard it from misapprehension and abuse ; hence he ceased to press it or proclaim it. Nevertheless he could not escape the odium which the subversive tenets and violent deeds of the rebels brought upon him, and this, when added to the odium generated by his deadly heresy, soon alienated from him all his early supporters and friends. John of Gaunt, the young King and his mother, the Council of Regency, the Parliament, all felt it impossible to continue to countenance a man whose teachings tended toward revolution in this world and perdition in the next. The friars turned against him with transubstantial fury. The University of Oxford, which protected him as long as it dared, and followed him as far as it could, was at length forced to

---

[1] There is, as a matter of fact, no communism in Wycliffe's works. Those who have supposed that there is have merely—by giving a material meaning where Wycliffe intended a spiritual one—misinterpreted such passages as " Fidelis hominis totus mundus divitiarum est, infidelis autem nec obolus." In Wycliffe's view every Christian man ideally possesses everything. This is not communism. It is merely individualism gone mad.

stop, as it contemplated with horror the abysses of rationalism into which he was descending. Even of his own Poor
Priests—the Lollard preachers of the new revolt—the more
cultured leaders fell away and made their peace with the
Church. He was left at the end of his life a very lonely
man, in the midst of alienated friends and ravening foes.

How did he escape destruction? It is not easy to say.
Some of his biographers—for example, Foxe, the martyro-
logist, and Burrows, his quincentenary eulogist—evidently
regret that he was not called upon to make an edifying
termination at the stake. His story thus concluded would
have pointed a more effective moral of the sort which they
desired. The fact, however, remains that, stricken down
by paralysis in his church at Lutterworth, he died a natural
death on the last day of the year 1384. But, though he
was spared the fiery trial by martyrdom, his followers were
not. In 1382, amid the alarm caused by the Peasants'
Revolt and the horror generated by the Lollard attack
upon the sanctities of the Mass, Courtenay—now Archbishop in the place of Sudbury, murdered by the peasants
—was able to retrieve his discomfiture of 1378. Describing himself as *per totam nostram provinciam Cantaburiensis
Inquisitor hæreticæ pravitatis*, he summoned a synod to the
Blackfriars in London. As the result of eight sessions
(May 17 to July 12, 1382) he secured the condemnation
of twenty-four of Wycliffe's conclusions—ten as heretical,
fourteen as erroneous. Further, on May 26, 1382, he
obtained from the King and the Lords an ordinance ordering
the sheriffs throughout England to arrest, imprison, and
hand over to the bishops, any persons whom they might
accuse of heresy. Here, indeed, was the Inquisition in
full force. Fortunately for the liberties of the country,
the Commons, who had not been consulted, took alarm,

and when Parliament met in October they compelled the withdrawal of the obnoxious ordinance, saying in notable words: " It is not the intention of the Commons to be tried for heresy, nor to bind over themselves or their descendants to the prelates, more than their ancestors had been in time past." It is an interesting example of the instinctive English appeal to precedent (invented, if necessary, for the occasion). By a succession of such appeals, as has been remarked by Tennyson and others, English freedom has broadened down. In this instance, Courtenay, checked in his hope of commanding secular aid in his hunt for heresy, had to content himself with a royal writ authorising the bishops themselves to arrest heretics if they could catch them. But this was a far inferior concession ; for the bishops lacked the secular paraphernalia of the chase. All the same, he was able to exercise a pressure which before his death in 1396 laid Lollardy very low.

The accusations brought against the Lollards, however, were exclusively theological in character. Hence they lie outside our present sphere. All that now remains for us to do is first to attempt a summary of Wycliffe's social and political ideas, and secondly to form an estimate of his character and achievement.

VII

It has been remarked that all Wycliffe's significant activities lay within the last ten years of his life. If he had died in 1374 his name would have passed into complete oblivion ; even if he had lived but till 1378, with his works on dominion composed, he would have been recollected dimly and uncertainly, merely as a second and inferior Marsilio, *damnatæ memoriæ*. It was the enormous and feverish output of the years 1378-84 which made him an everlasting portent and a purging power. Not often does it happen that a man radically changes his profession, materially alters his mode of life, or effectively shakes the world out of its old form, when he is sixty years of age !

The political and social ideas of Wycliffe, therefore, formulated as they were for the most part during the penultimate period of his career, are not among those thoughts of his which have had the greatest influence upon mankind. They are in the main academic in character ; they are expressed in highly technical scholastic Latin ; they are obscure both in substance and in accidents. Nevertheless, one of them, viz., the doctrine of dominion, which was at the basis of them all, is recognised as an important and curious contribution to sociological theory. The only trouble is that no one can quite understand what the doctrine is, or on what principle Wycliffe applied it.[1] It was not, however, a doctrine original to Wycliffe. He had learned it from Fitzralph, Archbishop of Armagh, who had developed it in his conflicts with the friars ; while Fitzralph himself claimed for his views the venerable authority of St Bernard, St Augustine, and the Gospels. Only gradually, moreover, did Wycliffe unfold the doctrine of dominion. He was an ecclesiastical politician before he was a political philosopher. He arrived at theory by way of practice. His early utterances, therefore, are clearer than his later. Hence to understand him it is best to watch his ideas as they grew in the hothouse of circumstances and in the forcing-ground of political controversy.

[1] The best discussions of Wycliffe's doctrine of dominion are to be found in the following works : R. L. Poole, *Illustrations of the History of Mediæval Thought* ; W. W. Shirley, introduction to *Fasciculi Zizaniorum* ; R. L. Poole, preface to Wycliffe's *De Dominio Divino* ; R. L. Poole, *Wycliffe and Movements for Reform* ; W. A. Dunning, *History of Political Theories* ; G. V. Lechler, *John Wycliffe and his English Precursors.*

First and foremost, then, he was a *nationalist*. Brought up during the Hundred Years War, and at a time when the Papacy appeared to be merely a French institution, he seems to have had no conception of Christendom as a whole, or of a Universal Church; still less of a united Humanity. His ideal was a national State with a national Church subordinate to it. He spoke of endowments as given *non cuicunque ecclesiæ sed singulariter ecclesiæ Anglicanæ*. He ended by urging that the English Church should reassert its independence of Rome and should live *more Græcorum sub propriis legibus*. It was his nationalism and his exclusively insular patriotism which commended him to the court of Edward III, and caused him to be sent as the English champion to the Conference of Bruges.

Closely allied to his nationalism was his ' *étatism*.' In the exaltation of the State and the ascription to it of sovereignty his writings anticipated *The Prince* of Machiavelli, the *Republic* of Bodin, the *Von Weltlicher Oberkeit* of Luther, and *The Leviathan* of Hobbes.[1] He based the duty of obedience to the civil authorities, not on his abstract theory of dominion—this he reserved exclusively for ecclesiastical purposes—but on the clear commands of Scripture and on the unequivocal examples of Christ and the Apostles. He agreed with Augustine and the Fathers generally that the fall of man necessitated and caused the institution of the State.[2] He regarded it as part of the divine scheme to bring man back to righteousness. So emphatic appeared to him to be the inspired injunction to obey " the powers that be " on the ground that they were " ordained of God," that he held it to be obligatory on

---

[1] Note particularly *De Civili Dominio*, Book I, ch. xxviii, and the tract *De Dominis et Servis*.
[2] "Dominium civile est dominium occasione peccati humanitus institutum " (*De Civ. Dom.*, Book I, ch. xviii).

Christian men to reverence the authority of even wicked tyrants, even as St Paul reverenced the authority of Nero. Nay, he went so far as to say, in words which scandalised the elect, that in certain circumstances *Deus debet obedire diabolo*. As to the form of government : in a better state of affairs a theocracy such as that depicted in the Book of Judges would be the ideal ; but in the actual sinfulness of the world a strong monarchy was essential.[1]

Appendant to his ' *étatism* ' was his *Erastianism*. He was Erastian both in the exact and in the popular sense of the term. In the exact sense he was Erastian in that he held that persuasion and not force was the proper method of the Church. In the popular sense, also, he was Erastian in that he held that the State was omnicompetent, having authority in all causes whether temporal or spiritual. This latter view — which Professor Maitland rightly calls Byzantine rather than Erastian—was expressly set forth in his *De Officio Regis* (1379). It portrays and advocates a relation of Church and State essentially identical with that later established by Henry VIII : it displays the king as supreme over ecclesiastical persons, ecclesiastical property, ecclesiastical courts. It exalts the State as against the Church, even going so far as to say that the State represents the divinity of Christ, while the Church represents but His humanity. The king is God's vicar in the government of his people, and bishops derive whatever authority they may have through him and him alone. This is more than even Hooker urged.[2]

From this extreme utterance it will be further evident that Wycliffe was not merely an Erastian but also an *anti-*

---

[1] See *De Civili Dominio*, Book I, ch. xxvi and xxvii.
[2] The following is a significant passage from the *De Officio Regis* (ch. vi) : " Episcopi, sui officiales et curati sui, tenentur in qualicunque tali causa spiritualiter cognoscere auctoritate regis ; ergo rex per illos. Sunt enim tales legii homines regis."

sacerdotalist. His mind, for all its mediæval trappings, was essentially the lay mind. It instinctively revolted against all the pretensions of priestly authority. It was the Renaissance mind not yet disentangled from the meshes of scholasticism. It came to the conclusion that the root of all sacerdotal superstition lay in the illusion that a person upon whom episcopal hands had been placed was anything which a layman was not; or could do anything which a layman could not do. This conclusion led inevitably to the repudiation of the whole sacramental system, and particularly to the denial of transubstantiation—that daily miracle of the Mass, the performance of which raised the lowest priest above the highest king.

Wycliffe's anti-sacerdotalism was only another aspect of his intense *individualism.* Wholly abandoning the common mediæval conception of the Church as an ark manned by a clerical crew busily engaged in rescuing a perishing humanity from a devil-infested flood, he reverted to the Augustinian idea of the Church as the communion of the elect, known only to God, and bound each one of them immediately to his Maker by the personal tie of grace. This indeed was the vital principle which underlay the obscure verbiage of the doctrine of dominion. Every man who rightfully exercised any authority or possessed any property held it directly, without any intervening lords, from the supreme *Dominus Capitalis,* the Creator of the Universe, to whom alone properly belonged all might, majesty, dominion, and power.

Wycliffe's individualism—perhaps his most remarkable characteristic in that age of old-established collectivism—was intimately associated with a *passion for righteousness.* The theory of dominion was not only a theory of personal relation; it was also a theory of moral responsibility.

The condition under which every creature held property and power from God was obedience to His holy will. Hence mortal sin entailed entire forfeiture. *Peccans mortaliter non habet dominium* was one of his striking sayings ; and, again, he contended *quod nullus existens in peccato mortali est dominus, sacerdos, vel episcopus,* and even *quod si papa sit præscitus et malus homo ac per consequens membrum diaboli, non habet potestatem supra fideles Christi ab aliquo sibi datam, nisi* [shades of Innocent IV and Boniface VIII !] *forte a Cæsare.* Here again was another blow at the sacerdotal system. For who could tell where and how often by mortal sin the chain of sacramental efficacy had been broken ? The truth seems to be that nothing scandalised Wycliffe's righteous soul more in that sinful age than the dissociation of religion from ethics, and the spectacle of corrupt priests (whose every act proclaimed their devotion to the world, the flesh, and the devil) maintaining that the validity of their official performances was not affected by their unofficial depravities. "By life been preestes known," he contended.

This brings us to another prominent article of Wycliffe's creed, viz., his strong and reiterated insistence on the *duty of the clergy to withdraw themselves from secular concerns and to surrender their mundane possessions.* They were to give themselves to good works and sound teaching, and to live by the charity of their flocks. He dated the decadence of the Church from the day of the Donation of Constantine, when the devil " bi Silvestre preest of Rome brought in a new gile and moved the Emperour of Rome to endowe the Churche in this preest." He contended again and again that the spheres of clergy and laity are distinct and separate. The functions of the clergy are purely spiritual ; to them not *dominium* but *ministerium* is assigned as a duty ; they should abjure earthly lordship and devote themselves to the service of their flocks. So urgent did Wycliffe regard the divestment of the spirituality of their terrestrial endowments that he called loudly upon the secular lords, to whom mundane property and power had been committed as an inalienable trust, to strip the clergy of their entangling wealth, if they would not strip themselves thereof. The secular lords, headed by John of Gaunt, indicated their readiness to render this little service to their religious brethren.[1]

VIII

This sketch of Wycliffe is already too long. But it must not be brought to a close without some brief attempt to estimate the character and influence of the reformer. Much traversing of the dull and dreary wastes of Wycliffe's writing has brought me to the suspicion—I might even say the conviction—that Wycliffe was not a religious man at all. This, I submit, is also the opinion of the Christian world—the Catholic section of it explicitly; the Protestant section tacitly. For though 'Wycliffe Halls' may be founded for the training of Protestant clergy, no one dreams of studying Wycliffe's works therein; though 'Wycliffe Preachers' may be instituted to combat the teachings of Rome, no one of these preachers ever thinks of quoting a word that Wycliffe said; though 'Wycliffe Societies' may be founded to put the multitude of his manuscripts into print, no single tract is ever considered edifying enough for general circulation. In fact, two separate 'Wycliffe Societies' (1844 and 1884) have already languished in the effort to get people to read, or even to buy, the soulless stuff he wrote. Much of it, after five

[1] Two notable tracts on this topic are printed by F. D. Matthew in his *English Works of Wycliffe*, pp. 359–402 and pp. 405–457.

centuries, is still unprinted, and (probably to no one's loss) likely to remain so.

Wycliffe, it is true, dealt largely with religious topics, and quoted Scripture freely to his purpose. But that does not compel us to call him religious. He was an academic theologian, a scholastic philosopher, a thinker whose interest in his theme was purely moral and intellectual. He seems to have had no religious experience; no sense of sin; no consciousness of conversion; no assurance of salvation; no heart of love; no evident communion with God. He made no emotional appeal; he roused no spiritual response in the souls of those to whom his dry syllogisms were addressed. He was, indeed, a rationalist, born before his due season.[1] His affinities were with the eighteenth century, and in the eighteenth century not with John Wesley but with David Hume. If he had lived in the nineteenth century he would have been the head, not of the Evangelical Alliance, but of the Rationalist Press. His definition of revelation would have satisfied the French Encyclopædists: revelation to him was merely a higher power of reason—*lumen supernaturale est forma perfectiva luminis naturalis.*[2]

The motive force behind the enormous activities of his closing decade was antagonism to Rome. He was antipapal, anti-clerical, anti-monastic, anti-sacramental, all but anti-Christian. He was merely negative and destructive. His Bible was but a weapon of offence; his pamphlets were violent polemics; his Poor Priests were not evangelists but revolutionary agitators. The hungry sheep whom temporarily he drew from their old pastures looked up to him and were not fed; and most of such as did not perish in their disillusionment made their way back to the fold where at

---

[1] To Wycliffe, though in a non-Hegelian sense, the real was the rational, and the rational the real.
[2] *De Dominio Divino*, Book I, ch. xi.

JOHN WYCLIFFE

any rate some scanty nutriment could begained. Wycliffe belonged to the Renaissance rather than to the Reformation. Not, of course, to the Renaissance of Southern Europe with its art, its poetry, its music, its soft and tender humanities ; but to the Renaissance of Northern Europe with its passion for truth, its instinct for science, its anarchic freedom, its stern zeal for righteousness.

He was a dour fighter, and he had to contend against foes of limitless malignity and power. To stand, as he did at the end of his life, almost solitary yet entirely un-dismayed, in the midst of enemies so many, so merciless, and so mighty, argues a courage little less than sublime. That he failed to appreciate the good qualities of his opponents was in the circumstances natural. It no doubt is difficult rightly to estimate the virtues of people who are plotting your destruction in this world and predicting your perdition in the next. Nevertheless it is regrettable that he should have called the clergy "fiends of hell," without recognising the greatness of the work which they had accomplished in civilising mediæval Europe ; and that he should have denounced the monks as "gluttonous idolaters" without taking into account all that the monas-teries had stood for through long centuries of rapine and war. Above all, it is regrettable that in his far-sighted anticipations of the remote future, with its national states, its Erastian churches, its autocratic monarchs, and its civil clergy, his very modern mind should have had so small a conception of the grandeur of those mediæval ideals of the Christian Commonwealth and the Church Universal which had filled the vision and inspired the pens of thinkers such as St Thomas Aquinas and dreamers such as Dante.

THE EDITOR

BIBLIOGRAPHY

A. Primary Sources

WYCLIFFE : *De Dominio Divino.* Ed. Poole, 1890.
    De Civili Dominio. Ed. Poole and Loserth, 1885–1905.
    De Ecclesia. Ed. Loserth, 1886.
    De Officio Regis. Ed. Pollard and Sayle, 1887.
    English Works. Ed. Matthew, 1880.
Fasciculi Zizaniorum. Ed. Shirley, 1858.
Concilia Magnæ Britanniæ. Ed. Wilkins, 1736.

B. Secondary Sources

BIGG, C. : *Wayside Sketches.* 1906.
BROWN, E. (editor) : *Fasciculus Rerum Expetendarum et Fugiendarum.* 1690.
BUDDENSIEG, R. : *Johann Wiclif und seine Zeit.* 1885.
CAPES, W. W. : *The English Church in the Fourteenth and Fifteenth Centuries.* 1900.
CREIGHTON, M. : *History of the Papacy*, vol. i. 2nd edition, 1897.
CREIGHTON, M. : *Historical Essays and Reviews.* Ed. L. Creighton, 1902.
DUNNING, W. A. : *A History of Political Theories, Ancient and Mediæval.* 1910.
FIGGIS, J. N. : "John Wyclif" in *Typical English Churchmen*, Second Series, 1909.
LECHLER, G. V. (translated by P. Lorimer) : *John Wycliffe and his English Precursors.* 1878.
LEWIS, J. : *Life of Wicliffe.* 1720.
LOSERTH, J. : Article "Wiclif" in Herzog-Hauck, *Realencyklopädie.*
LYTE, H. C. M. : *History of the University of Oxford.* 1886.
POOLE, R. L. : *Illustrations of the History of Mediæval Thought and Learning.* 2nd edition, 1920.
POOLE, R. L. : *Wycliffe and the Movements for Reform.* 1888.
POOLE, R. L. : Article "Wyclif" in *Encyclopædia Britannica.* 1911.
RASHDALL, H. : *The Universities of the Middle Ages.* 1895.
RASHDALL, H. : Article "John Wycliffe" in *Dictionary of National Biography.* 1900.
SERGEANT, L. : *John Wyclif.* 1893.
TREVELYAN, G. M. : *England in the Age of Wycliffe.* 1899.
VAUGHAN, R. : *Life and Opinions of Wycliffe.* 1828.
WORKMAN, H. B. : *The Dawn of the Reformation*, vol. i. 1901.

H. A. IRONSIDE
MEMORIAL LIBRARY